I0865841

Prejudices:
Second Series

H. L. Mencken

CONTENTS

SECOND SERIES

I. THE NATIONAL LETTERS

1. Prophets and Their Visions

IT is convenient to begin, like the gentlemen of God, with a glance at a text or two. The first, a short one, is from Ralph Waldo Emerson's celebrated oration, "The American Scholar," delivered before the Phi Beta Kappa Society at Cambridge on August 31st, 1837. Emerson was then thirtyfour years old and almost unknown in his own country, though he had already published "Nature" and established his first contacts with Landor and Carlyle. But "The American Scholar" brought him into instant notice at home, partly as man of letters but more importantly as seer and prophet, and the fame thus founded has endured without much diminution, at all events in New. England, to this day. Oliver Wendell Holmes, giving words to what was undoubtedly the common feeling, hailed the address as the intellectual declaration of independence of the American people, and that judgment, amiably passed on by three generations of pedagogues, still survives in the literature books. I quote from the first paragraph:

Our day of dependence, our long apprenticeship to the learning of other lands, draws to a close. . . . Events, actions arise, that must be sung, that will sing themselves. Who can doubt that poetry will revive and lead in a new age, as the star in the constellation Harp, which now flames in our zenith, astronomers announce, shall one day be the pole-star for a thousand years?

This, as I say, was in 1837. Thirty-three years later, in 1870, Walt Whitman echoed the prophecy in his even more famous "Democratic Vistas." What he saw in his vision and put into his gnarled and gasping prose was

a class of native authors, literatuses, far different, far higher in grade, than any yet known, sacerdotal, modern, fit to cope with our occasions, lands, permeating the whole mass of American morality, taste, belief, breathing into it a new breath of life, giving it decision, affecting politics far more than the popular superficial suffrage, with results inside and underneath the elections of Presidents or Congress — radiating, begetting appropriate teachers, schools, manners, and, as its grandest result, accomplishing, (what neither the schools nor the churches and their clergy have hitherto accomplished, and without which this nation will no more stand, permanently, soundly, than a house will stand without a substratum,) a religious and moral character beneath the political and productive and intellectual bases of the States.

And out of the vision straightway came the prognostication: The promulgation and belief in such a class or order — a new and greater literatus order — its possibility, (nay, certainty,) underlies these entire speculations. . . . Above all previous lands, a great original literature is sure to become the justification and reliance, (in some respects the sole reliance,) of American democracy.

Thus Whitman in 1870, the time of the first draft of "Democratic Vistas." He was of the same mind, and said so, in 1888, four years before his death. I could bring up texts of like tenor in great number, from the years before 1837, from those after 1888, and from every decade between. The dream of Emerson, though the eloquence of its statement was new and arresting, embodied no novel projection of the fancy; it merely gave a sonorous *Waldhorn* tone to what had been dreamed and said before. You will find almost the same high hope, the same exuberant confidence in the essays of the elder Channing and in the "Lectures on American Literature" of Samuel Lorenzo Knapp, LL.D., the first native critic of beautiful letters — the primordial tadpole of all our later Mores, Brownells, Phelpses, Mabies, Brander Matthewses and other such grave and glittering fish. Knapp believed, like Whitman long after him, that the sheer physical grandeur of the New World would inflame a race of bards to unprecedented utterance. "What are the Tibers and Scamanders," he demanded, "measured by the Missouri and the Amazon? Or what the loveliness of Illysus or Avon by the Connecticut or the Potomack? Whenever a nation wills it, prodigies are born." That is to s ay, prodigies literary and ineffable as well as purely material — prodigies aimed, in his own words, at "the olympick crown" as well as at mere railroads, ships, wheat-fields, droves of hogs, factories and money. Nor were Channing and Knapp the first of the haruspices. Noah Webster, the lexicographer, who "taught millions to spell but not one to sin," had seen the early starlight of the same Golden Age so early as 1789, as the curious will find by examining his "Dissertations on the English Language," a work fallen long since into undeserved oblivion. Nor was Whitman, taking sober second thought exactly a century later, the last of them. Out of many brethren of our own day, extravagantly articulate in print and among the chautauquas, I choose one — not because his hope is of purest water, but precisely because, like Emerson, he dilutes it with various discreet whereases. He is Van Wyck Brooks, a young man far more intelligent, penetrating and hospitable to fact than any of the reigning professors — a critic who is sharply differentiated from them, indeed, by the simple circumstance that he has information and sense. Yet this extraordinary Mr. Brooks, in his "Letters and Leadership," published in 1918, rewrites "The American Scholar" in terms borrowed almost bodily from "Democratic Vistas" — that is to say, he prophesies with Emerson and exults with Whitman. First there is the Emersonian doctrine of the soaring individual made articulate by freedom and realizing "the responsibility that lies upon us, each in the measure of his own gift." And then there is Whitman's vision of a self -interpretative democracy, forced into high literary adventures by Joseph Conrad's "obscure inner necessity," and so achieving a "new synthesis adaptable to the unique conditions of our life." And finally there is the specific prediction, the grandiose, Adam Forepaugh mirage: "We shall become a luminous people, dwelling in the light and sharing our light." . . .

As I say, the roll of such soothsayers might be almost endlessly lengthened. There is, in truth, scarcely a formal discourse upon the national letters (forgetting, perhaps, Barrett Wendell's sour threnody upon the New England Aufklarung) that is without some touch of this previsional exultation, this confident hymning of glories to come, this fine assurance that American literature, in some future always ready to dawn, will burst into so grand a flowering that history will cherish its loveliest blooms even above such salient American gifts to culture as the moving-picture, the phonograph, the New Thought and the bichloride tablet. If there was ever a dissenter from the national optimism, in this as in other departments, it was surely Edgar Allan Poe — without question the bravest and most original, if perhaps also the least orderly and judicious, of all the critics that we have produced. And yet even Poe, despite his general habit of disgust and dismay, caught a flash or two of that engaging picture — even Poe, for an instant, in 1846, thought that he saw the beginnings of a solid and autonomous native literature, its roots deep in the soil of the republic — as you will discover by turning to his forgotten essay on J. G. C. Brainard, a thrice-forgotten doggereleer of Jackson's time. Poe, of course, was too cautious to let his imagination proceed to details; one feels that a certain doubt, a saving peradventure or two, played about the unaccustomed vision as he beheld it. But, nevertheless, he unquestionably beheld it....

2. The Answering Fact

Now for the answering fact. How has the issue replied to these visionaries? It has replied in a way that is manifestly to the discomfiture of Emerson as a prophet, to the dismay of Poe as a pessimist disarmed by transient optimism, and to the utter collapse of Whitman. We have, as every one knows, produced no such "new and greater literatus order" as that announced by old Walt. We have given a gaping world no books that "radiate," and surely none intelligibly comparable to stars and constellations. We have achieved no prodigies of the first class, and very few of the second class, and not many of the third and fourth classes. Our literature, despite several false starts that promised much, is chiefly remarkable, now as always, for its respectable mediocrity. Its typical great man, in our own time, has been Howells, as its typical great man a generation ago was Lowell, and two generations ago, Irving. Viewed largely, its salient character appears as a sort of timorous flaccidity, an amiable hollowness. In bulk it grows more and more formidable, in ease and decorum it makes undoubted progress, and on the side of mere technic, of the bald capacity to write, it shows an ever-widening competence. But when one proceeds from such agencies and externals to the intrinsic substance, to the creative passion within, that substance quickly reveals itself as thin and watery, and that passion fades to something almost puerile. In all that mass of suave and often highly diverting writing there is no visible movement toward a distinguished and singular excellence, a signal national quality, a ripe and stimulating flavor, or, indeed, toward any other describable goal. What one sees is simply a general irresolution, a pervasive superficiality. There is no sober grappling with fundamentals, but only a shy sporting on the surface; there is not even any serious approach, such as Whitman dreamed of, to the special experiences and emergencies of the American people. When one turns to any other national literature — to Russian literature, say, or French, or German or Scandinavian — one is conscious immediately of a definite attitude toward the primary mysteries of existence, the unsolved and ever-fascinating problems at the bottom of human life, and of a definite preoccupation with some of them, and a definite way of translating their challenge into drama. These attitudes and preoccupations raise a literature above mere poetizing and tale-telling; they give it dignity and importance; above all, they give it national character. But it is precisely here that the literature of America, and especially the later literature, is most colorless and inconsequential. As if paralyzed by the national fear of ideas, the democratic distrust of whatever strikes beneath the prevailing platitudes, it evades all resolute and honest dealing with what, after all, must be every healthy literature's elementary materials. One is conscious of no brave and noble earnestness in it, of no generalized passion for intellectual and spiritual adventure, of no organized determination to think things out. What is there is a highly self-conscious and insipid correctness, a bloodiless respectability, a submergence of matter in manner — in brief, what is there is the feeble, uninspiring quality of German painting and English music.

It was so in the great days and it is so today. There has always been hope and there has always been failure. Even the most optimistic prophets of future glories have been united, at all times, in their discontent with the here and now, "The mind of this country," said Emerson, speaking of what was currently visible in 1837, "is taught to aim at low objects. . . . There is no work for any but the decorous and the complaisant. . . Books are written . . by men of talent . . . who start wrong, who set out from accepted dogmas, not from their own sight of principles." And then, turning to the way out: "The office of the scholar (i.e., of Whitman's 'literatus') is to cheer, to raise and to guide men by showing them facts amid appearances." Whitman himself, a full generation later, found that office still unfilled. "Our fundamental want today in the United States," he said, "with closest, amplest reference to present conditions, and to the future, is of a class, and the clear idea of a class, of native authors, literatuses, far different, far higher in grade, than any yet known" — and so on, as I have already quoted him. And finally, to make an end of the prophets, there is Brooks, with nine-tenth's of his book given over, not to his prophecy — it is crowded, indeed, into the last few pages — but to a somewhat heavy mourning over the actual scene before him. On the side of letters, the aesthetic side, the side of ideas, we present to the world at large, he says, "'the spectacle of a vast, undifferentiated herd of good-humored animals" — Knights of Pythias, Presbyterians, standard model Ph.D.'s, readers of the Saturday Evening Post" admirers of Richard Harding Davis and

o. Henry, devotees of Hamilton Wright Mabie's "white list" of books, members of the Y. M, C. A. or the Drama League, weepers at chautauquas, wearers of badges, 100 per cent, patriots, children of God, Poe I pass over; I shall turn to him again later on. Nor shall I repeat the parrotings of Emerson and Whitman in the jeremiads of their innumerable heirs and assigns. What they all establish is what is already obvious: that American thinking, when it concerns itself with beautiful letters as when it concerns itself with religious dogma or political theory, is extraordinarily timid and superficial — that it evades the genuinely serious problems of life and art as if they were stringently taboo— -that the outward virtues it undoubtedly shows are always the virtues, not of profundity, not of courage, not of originality, but merely those of an emasculated and often very trashy dilettantism.

3. The Ashes of New England

The current scene is surely depressing enough. What one observes is a literature in three layers, and each inordinately doughy and uninspiring — each almost without flavor or savor. It is hard to say, with much critical plausibility, which layer deserves to be called the upper, but for decorum's sake the choice may be fixed upon that which meets with the approval of the reigning Lessings. This is the layer of the novels of the late Howells, Judge Grant, Alice Brown and the rest of the dwindling survivors of New England Kultur, of the brittle, academic poetry of Woodberry and the elder Johnson, of the tea-party essays of Crothers, Miss Repplier and company, and of the solemn, highly judicial, coroner's inquest criticism of More, Brownell, Babbitt and their imitators. Here we have manner, undoubtedly. The thing is correctly done; it is never crude or gross; there is in it a faint perfume of college-town society. But when this highly refined and attenuated manner is allowed for what remains is next to nothing. One never remembers a character in the novels of these aloof and de-Americanized Americans; one never encounters an idea in their essays; one never carries away a line out of their poetry. It is literature as an academic exercise for talented grammarians, almost as a genteel recreation for ladies and gentlemen of fashion — the exact equivalent, in the field of letters, of eighteenth century painting and German Augenmusik.

What ails it, intrinsically, is a dearth of intellectual audacity and of aesthetic passion. Running through it, and characterizing the work of almost every man and woman producing it, there is an unescapable suggestion of the old Puritan suspicion of the fine arts as such — of the doctrine that they offer fit asylum for good citizens only when some ulterior and superior purpose is carried into them. This purpose, naturally enough, most commonly shows a moral tinge. The aim of poetry, it appears, is to fill the mind with lofty thoughts — not to give it joy, but to give it a grand and somewhat gaudy sense of virtue. The essay is a weapon against the degenerate tendencies of the age. The novel, properly conceived, is a means of uplifting the spirit; its aim is to inspire, not merely to satisfy the low curiosity of man in man. The Puritan, of course, is not entirely

5

devoid of aesthetic feeling. He has a taste for good form; he responds to style; he is even capable of something approaching a purely aesthetic emotion. But he fears this aesthetic emotion as an insinuating distraction from his chief business in life: the sober consideration of the all-important problem of conduct. Art is a temptation, a seduction, a Lorelei, and the Good Man may safely have traffic with it only when it is broken to moral uses — in other words, when its innocence is pumped out of it, and it is purged of gusto. It is precisely this gusto that one misses in all the work of the New England school, and in all the work of the formal schools that derive from it. One observes in such a fellow as Dr. Henry Van Dyke an excellent specimen of the whole clan. He is, in his way, a genuine artist. He has a hand for pretty verses. He wields a facile rhetoric. He shows, in indiscreet moments, a touch of imagination. But all the while he remains a sound Presbyterian, with one eye on the devil. He is a Presbyterian first and an artist second, which is just as comfortable as trying to be a Presbyterian first and a chorus girl second. To such a man it must inevitably appear that a Moliere, a Wagner, a Goethe or a Shakespeare was more than a little bawdy.

The criticism that supports this decaying caste of literary Brahmins is grounded almost entirely upon ethical criteria. You will spend a long while going through the works of such typical professors as More, Phelps, Boynton, Burton, Perry, Brownell and Babbitt before ever you encounter a purely aesthetic judgment upon an aesthetic question. It is almost as if a man estimating daffodils should do it in terms of artichokes. Phelps' whole body of "we churchgoers" criticism — the most catholic and tolerant, it may be said in passing, that the faculty can show — consists chiefly of a plea for correctness, and particularly for moral correctness; he never gets very far from "the axiom of the moral law." Brownell argues eloquently for standards that would bind an imaginative author as tightly as a Sunday-school superintendent is bound by the Ten Commandments and the Mann Act. Sherman tries to save Shakespeare for the right-thinking by proving that he was an Iowa Methodist — a member of his local Chamber of Commerce, a contemner of Reds, an advocate of democracy and the League of Nations, a patriotic dollar-a-year-man during the Armada scare. Elmer More devotes himself, year in and year out, to denouncing the Romantic movement, i. e., the effort to emancipate the artist from formulae and categories, and so make him free to dance with arms and legs. And Babbitt, to make an end, gives over his days and his nights to deploring Rousseau's anarchistic abrogation of "the veto power" over the imagination, leading to such "wrongness" in both art and life that it threatens "to wreck civilization." In brief, the alarms of schoolmasters. Not many of them deal specifically with the literature that is in being. It is too near to be quite nice. To More or Babbitt only death can atone for the primary offense of the artist. But what they preach nevertheless has its echoes contemporaneously, and those echoes, in the main, are woefully falsetto. I often wonder what sort of picture of These States is conjured up by foreigners who read, say, Crothers, Van Dyke, Babbitt, the later Winston Churchill, and the old maids of the Freudian suppression school. How can such a foreigner, moving in those damp, asthmatic mists, imagine such phenomena as Roosevelt, Billy Sunday, Bryan, the Becker case, the I. W. W., Newport, Palm Beach, the University of Chicago, Chicago itself — the whole, gross, glittering, excessively dynamic, infinitely grotesque, incredibly stupendous drama of American life?

As I have said, it is not often that the *ordentlichen Professoren* deign to notice contemporary writers, even of their own austere kidney. In all the Shelburne Essays there is none on Howells, or on Churchill, or on Mrs. Wharton; More seems to think of American literature as expiring with Longfellow and Donald G. Mitchell. He has himself hinted that in the department of criticism of criticism there enters into the matter something beyond mere aloof ignorance. "I soon learned (as editor of the pre-Bolshevik Nation)" he says, "that it was virtually impossible to get fair consideration for a book written by a scholar not connected with a university from a reviewer so connected." This class consciousness, however, should not apply to artists, who are admittedly inferior to professors, and it surely does not show itself in such men as Phelps and Spingarn, who seem to be very eager to prove that they are not professorial. Yet Phelps, in the course of a long work on the novel, pointedly omits all mention of such men as Dreiser, and Spingarn, as the aforesaid Brooks has said, "appears to be less inclined even than the critics with whom he is theoretically at war to play an active public part in the secular conflict of darkness and light" When one comes to the Privat-Dozenten there is less remoteness, but what takes the place of it is almost as saddening. To Sherman and Percy Boynton the one aim of criticism seems to be the enforcement of correctness — in Emerson's phrase, the upholding of 'some great decorum, some fetish of a government, some ephemeral trade, or war, or man" — e. g., Puritanism, democracy, monogamy, the League of Nations, the Wilsonian piffle. Even among the critics who escape the worst of this school-mastering frenzy there is some touch of the heavy "culture" of the provincial schoolma'm. For example, consider Clayton Hamilton, M.A., vice-president of the National Institute of Arts and Letters. Here are the tests he proposes for dramatic critics, u e., for gentlemen chiefly employed in reviewing such characteristic American compositions as the Ziegfeld Follies, "Up m Mabel's Room," "Ben-Hur" and "The Witching Hour":

1. Have you ever stood bareheaded in the nave of Amiens?

2. Have you ever climbed to the Acropolis by moonlight?

3. Have you ever walked with whispers into the hushed presence of the Frari Madonna of Bellini?

What could more brilliantly evoke an image of the eternal Miss Birch, blue veil flying and Baedeker in hand, plodding along faithfully through the interminable corridors and catacombs of the Louvre, the while bands are playing across the river, and young bucks in three-gallon hats are sparking the gals, and the Jews and harlots uphold the traditions of French *hig leef* at Longchamps, and American deacons are frisked and debauched up on martyrs' hill? The banality of it is really too exquisite to be borne; the lack of humor is almost that of a Fifth avenue divine. One seldom finds in the pronunciamentoes of these dogged professors, indeed, any trace of either Attic or Gallic salt When they essay to be jocose, the result is usually simply an elephantine whimsicality, by the *chautauqua* out of the Atlantic Monthly. Their satire is mere ill-nature. One finds it difficult to believe that they have ever read Lewes, or Hazlitt, or, above all, Saintsbury. I often wonder, in fact, how Saintsbury would fare, an unknown man, at the hands of, say, Brownell or More. What of his iconoclastic gayety, his boyish weakness for tweaking noses and pulling whiskers, his obscene delight in slang? . . .

4. The Ferment Underground

So much for the top layer. The bottom layer is given over to the literature of Greenwich Village, and by Greenwich Village, of course, I mean the whole of the advanced wing in letters, whatever the scene of its solemn declarations of independence and forlorn hopes. Miss Amy Lowell is herself a fully-equipped and automobile Greenwich Village, domiciled in Boston amid the crumbling gravestones of the New England *intelligentsia,* but often in waspish joy-ride through the hinterland. Vachel Lindsay, with his pilgrim's staff, is another. There is a third in Chicago, with Poetry: A Magazine of Verse as its Exhibit A; it is, in fact, the senior of the Village fornenst Washington Square. Others you will find in far-flung factory towns, wherever there is a Little Theater, and a couple of local Synges and Chekovs to supply its stage. St. Louis, before Zoe Akins took flight, had the busiest of all these Greenwiches, and the most interesting. What lies under the whole movement is the natural revolt of youth against the pedagogical Prussianism of the professors. The oppression is extreme, and so the rebellion is extreme. Imagine a sentimental young man of the provinces, awaking one morning to the somewhat startling discovery that he is full of the divine afflatus, and nominated by the hierarchy of hell to enrich the literature of his fatherland. He seeks counsel and aid. He finds, on consulting the official treatises on that literature, that its greatest poet was Longfellow. He is warned, reading More and Babbitt, that the literatus who lets feeling get into his compositions is a psychic fornicator, and under German influences. He has formal notice from Sherman that Puritanism is the lawful philosophy of the country, and that any dissent from it is treason. He gets the news, plowing through the New York Times Book Review, the Nation (so far to the left in its politics, but hugging the right so desperately in letters!) the Bookman, the Atlantic and the rest, that the salient artists of the living generation are such masters as Robert Underwood Johnson, Owen Wister, James Lane Allen, George E. Woodberry, Hamlin Garland, William Roscoe Thayer and Augustus Thomas, with polite bows to Margaret Deland, Mary Johnston and Ellen Glasgow. It slowly dawns upon him that Robert W. Chambers is an academician and Theodore Dreiser isn't, that Brian Hooker is and George Sterling isn't, that Henry Sydnor Harrison is and James Branch Cabell isn't, that "Chimmie Fadden" Townsaid is and Sherwood Anderson isn't.

Is it any wonder that such a young fellow, after one or two sniffs of that prep-school fog, swings so vastly backward that one finds him presently in corduroy trousers and a velvet jacket, hammering furiously upon a pine table in a Macdougal street cellar, his mind full of malicious animal magnetism against even so amiable an old maid as Howells, and his discourse full of insane hair-splittings about vers libre, futurism, spectrism, vorticism, *Expressionismus, heliogabalisme*? The thing, in truth, is in the course of nature. The Spaniards who were outraged by the Palmerism of Torquemada did not become members of the Church of England; they became atheists. The American colonists, in revolt against a bad king, did not set up a good king; they set up a democracy, and so gave every honest man a chance to become a rogue on his own account. Thus the young literatus, emerging from the vacuum of Ohio or Arkansas. An early success, as we shall see, tends to halt and moderate him. He finds that, after all, there is still a place for him, a sort of asylum for such as he, not over-populated or very warmly-heated, but nevertheless quite real. But if his sledding at the start is hard, if the corrective birch finds him while he is still tender, then he goes, as Andrew Jackson would say, the whole hog, and another voice is added to the raucous bellowing of the literary Reds.

I confess that the spectacle gives me some joy, despite the fact that the actual output of the Village is seldom worth noticing. What commonly engulfs and spoils the Villagers is their concern with mere technique. Among them, it goes without saying, are a great many frauds — poets whose yearning to write is unaccompanied by anything properly describable as capacity, dramatists whose dramas are simply Schnitzler and well-water, workers in prose fiction who gravitate swiftly and inevitably to the machine-made merchandise of the cheap magazines — in brief.

American equivalents of the bogus painters of the Boul' Mich'. These pretenders, having no ideas, naturally try to make the most of forms. Half the wars in the Village are over form; content is taken for granted, or forgotten altogether. The extreme leftists, in fact, descend to a meaningless gibberish, both in prose and in verse; it is their last defiance to intellectualism. This childish concentration upon externals unfortunately tends to debauch the small minority that is of more or less genuine parts; the good are pulled in by the bad. As a result, the Village produces nothing that justifies all the noise it makes. I have yet to hear of a first-rate book coming out of it, or a short story of arresting quality, or even a poem of any solid distinction. As one of the editors of a magazine which specializes in the work of new authors I am in an exceptional position to report. Probably nine-tenths of the stuff written in the dark dens and alleys south of the arch comes to my desk soon or late, and I go through all of it faithfully. It is, in the overwhelming main, jejune and imitative. The prose is quite without distinction, either in matter or in manner. The verse seldom gets beyond a hollow audaciousness, not unlike that of cubist painting. It is not often, indeed, that even personality is in it; all of the Villagers seem to write alike. "Unless one is an expert in some detective method," said a recent writer in Poetry " "one is at a loss to assign correctly the ownership of much free verse—

9

that is, if one plays fairly and refuses to look at the signature until one has ventured a guess. It is difficult, for instance, to know whether Miss Lowell is writing Mr. Bynner's verse, or whether he is writing hers." Moreover, this monotony keeps to a very low level. There is no poet in the movement who has produced anything even remotely approaching the fine lyrics of Miss Reese, Miss Teasdale and John McClure, and for all its war upon the cliche it can show nothing to equal the cliche-free beauty of Robert Loveman's "Rain Song." In the drama the Village has gone further. In Eugene "Neill, Rita Wellman and Zoe Akins it offers dramatists who are obviously many cuts above the well-professored mechanicians who pour out of Prof. Dr. Baker's Ibsenfabrik at Cambridge. But here we must probably give the credit, not to any influence residing within the movement itself, but to mere acts of Cod. Such pieces as "Neill's one-acters, Miss Wellman's "The Centile Wife" and Miss Akins' extraordinary "Papa" lie quite outside the Village scheme of things. There is no sign of formal revolt in them. They are simply first-rate work, done miraculously in a third-rate land. But if the rebellion is thus sterile of direct results, and, in more than one aspect, fraudulent and ridiculous, it is at all events an evidence of something not to be disregarded, and that something is the gradual formulation of a challenge to the accepted canons in letters and to the accepted canon lawyers. The first hoots come from a tatterdemalion horde of rogues and vagabonds without the gates, but soon or late, let us hope, they will be echoed in more decorous quarters, and with much greater effect. The Village, in brief, is an earnest that somewhere or other new seeds are germinating. Between the young tutor who launches into letters with imitations of his seminary chief's imitations of Agnes Repplier's imitations of Charles Lamb, and the young peasant who tries to get his honest exultations into free verse there can be no hesitant choice: the peasant is, by long odds, the sounder artist, and, what is more, the sounder American artist. Even the shy and somewhat stagey carnality that characterizes the Village has its high symbolism and its profound uses. It proves that, despite repressions unmatched in civilization in modern times, there is still a sturdy animality in American youth, and hence good health. The poet hugging his Sonia in a Washington square beanery, and so giving notice to all his world that he is a devil of a fellow, is at least a better man than the emasculated stripling in a Y. M. C. A. gospel-mill, pumped dry of all his natural appetites and the vacuum filled with double-entry book-keeping, business economics and autoerotism. In so foul a nest of imprisoned and fermenting sex as the United States, plain fornication becomes a mark of relative decency.

5. In the Literary Abattoir

But the theme is letters, not wickedness. The upper and lower layers have been surveyed. There remains the middle layer, the thickest and perhaps the most significant of the three. By the middle layer I mean the literature that fills the magazines and burdens the book-counters in the department-stores — the literature adorned by such artists as Richard Harding Davis, Rex Beach, Emerson Hough, O. Henry, James Whitcomb Riley, Augustus Thomas, Robert

W. Chambers, Henry Sydnor Harrison, Owen Johnson, Cyrus Townsend Brady, Irvin Cobb and Mary Roberts Rinehart — in brief, the literature that pays like a bucket-shop or a soap-factory, and is thus thoroughly American. At the bottom this literature touches such depths of banality that it would be difficult to match it in any other country. The "inspirational" and patriotic essays of Dr. Frank Crane, Orison Sweet Marden, Porter Emerson Browne, Gerald Stanley Lee, E. S. Martin, Ella Wheeler Wilcox and the Rev. Dr. Newell Dwight Hillis, the novels of Harold Bell Wright, Eleanor H. Porter and Gene Stratton-Porter, and the mechanical sentimentalities in prose and verse that fill the cheap fiction magazines — this stuff has a native quality that is as unmistakable as that of Mother's Day, Billy Sundayism or the Junior Order of United American Mechanics. It is the natural outpouring of a naive and yet half barbarous people, full of delight in a few childish and inaccurate ideas. But it would be a grave error to assume that the whole of the literature of the middle layer is of the same infantile quality. On the contrary, a great deal of it — for example, the work of Mrs. Rinehart, and that of Corra Harris, Gouverneur Morris, Harold MacGrath and the late o. Henry — shows an unmistakably technical excellence, and even a certain civilized sophistication in point of view. Moreover, this literature is constantly graduating adept professors into something finer, as witness Booth Tarkington, Zona Gale, Ring W. Lardner and Montague Glass. S. L. Clemens came out of forty years ago. Nevertheless, its general tendency is distinctly in the other direction. It seduces by the power of money, and by the power of great acclaim no less. One constantly observes the collapse and surrender of writers who started out with aims far above that of the magazine nabob. I could draw up a long, long list of such victims: Henry Milner Rideout, Jack London, Owen Johnson, Chester Bailey Femald, Hamlin Garland, Will Levington Comfort, Stephen French Whitman, James Hopper, Harry Leon Wilson, and so on. They had their forerunner, in the last generation, in Bret Harte. It is, indeed, a characteristic American phenomenon for a young writer to score a success with novel and meritorious work, and then to yield himself to the bestseller fever, and so disappear down the sewers. Even the man who struggles to emerge again is commonly hauled back. For example, Louis Joseph Vance, Rupert Hughes, George Bronson-Howard, and, to go back a few years, David Graham Phillips and Elbert Hubbard — all men flustered by high aspiration, and yet all pulled down by the temptations below. Even Frank Norris showed signs of yielding. The pull is genuinely powerful. Above lies not only isolation, but also a dogged and malignant sort of opposition. Below, as Morris has frankly admitted, there is the place at Aiken, the motor-car, babies, money in the bank, and the dignity of an important man.

It is a commonplace of the envious to put all the blame upon the Saturday Evening Post, for in its pages many of the Magdalens of letters are to be found, and out of its bulging coffers comes much of the lure. But this is simply blaming the bull for the sins of all the cows. The Post, as a matter of fact, is a good deal less guilty than such magazines as the Cosmopolitan Hearsts, McClure's and the Metropolitan, not to mention the larger women's magazines. In the Post one often discerns an effort to rise above the level of shoe-drummer fiction. It is edited by a man who, almost alone among editors of the great periodicals of the country, is himself a writer of respectable skill. It has brought out (after lesser publications unearthed them) a member of authors of very solid talents, notably Glass, Lardner and E. W. Howe. It has been extremely hospitable to men not immediately comprehensible to the mob, for example, Dreiser and Hergesheimer. Most of all, it has avoided the Barnum-like exploitation of such native bosh-mongers as Crane, Hillis and Ella Wheeler Wilcox, and of such exotic mountebanks as D'Annunzio, Hall Caine and Maeterlinck. In brief, the Post is a great deal better than ever Greenwich Village and the Cambridge campus are disposed to admit. It is the largest of all the literary Hog Islands, but it is by no means the worst. Appealing primarily to the great masses of right-thinking and unintelligent Americans, it must necessarily print a great deal of preposterous tosh, but it flavors the mess with not a few things of a far higher quality, and at its worst it is seldom downright idiotic. In many of the other great magazines one finds stuff that it would be difficult to describe in any other words. It is gaudily romantic, furtively sexual, and full of rubber-stamp situations and personages — a sort of amalgam of the worst drivel of Marie Corelli, Elinor Glyn, E. Phillips Oppenheim, William Le Quex and Hall Caine. This is the literature of the middle layer — the product of the national Rockefellers and Duponts of letters. This is the sort of thing that the young author of facile pen is encouraged to manufacture. This is the material of the best sellers and the movies.

Of late it is the movies that have chiefly provoked its composition: the rewards they offer are even greater than those held out by the commercial book publishers and the train-boy magazines. The point of view of an author responsive to such rewards was recently set forth very naively in the Authors' League Bulletin. This author undertook, in a short article, to refute the fallacies of an unknown who ventured to protest against the movies on the ground that they called only for bald plots, elementary and generally absurd, and that all the rest of a sound writer's equipment — "the artistry of his style, the felicity of his apt expression, his subtlety and thoroughness of observation and comprehension and sympathy, the illuminating quality of his analysis of motive and character, even the fundamental skillful development of the bare plot" — was disdained by the Selznicks, Goldfishes, Zukors and other such entrepreneurs" and by the overwhelming majority of their customers. I quote from the reply:

There are some conspicuous word merchants who deal in the English language, but the general public doesn't clamor for their wares. They write for the "'thinking class." The elite, the discriminating. As a rule, they scorn the crass commercialism of the magazines and movies and such catchpenny devices. However, literary masterpieces live because they have been and will be read, not by the few, but by the many. That was true in the time of Homer, and even to-day the first move made by an editor when he receives a manuscript, or a gentle reader when he buys a book, or a T. B. M. when he sinks into an orchestra chair is to look around for John Henry Plot If Mr. Plot is too long delayed in arriving or doesn't come at all, the editor usually sends regrets, the reader yawns and the tired business man falls asleep. It's a sad state of affairs and awful tough on art, but it can't be helped.

Observe the lofty scorn of mere literature — the superior irony at the expense of everything beyond the bumping of boobs. Note the sound judgment as to the function and fate of literary masterpieces, e. g., "Endymion," "The Canterbury Tales," "Faust," "Typhoon." Give your eye to the chaste diction — "John Henry Plot," "T. B. M.," "awful tough," and so on. No doubt you will at once assume that this curious counterblast to literature was written by some former bartender now engaged in composing scenarios for Pearl White and Theda Bara. But it was not. It was written and signed by the president of the Authors' League of America.

Here we have, unconsciously revealed, the secret of the depressing badness of what may be called the staple fiction of the country — the sort of stuff that is done by the Richard Harding Davises, Rex Beaches, Houghs, McCutcheons, and their like, male and female. The worse of it is not that it is addressed primarily to shoe-drummers and shop-girls; the worst of it is that it is written by authors who are, to all intellectual intents and purposes, shoe-drummers and shop-girls. American literature, even on its higher levels, seldom comes out of the small and lonesome upper classes of the people. An American author with traditions behind him and an environment about him comparable to those, say, of George Moore, or Hugh Walpole, or E. F. Benson is and always has been relatively rare. On this side of the water the arts, like politics and religion, are chiefly in the keeping of persons of obscure origin, defective education and elemental tastes. Even some of the most violent upholders of the New England superstition are aliens to the actual New England heritage; one discovers, searching "Who's Who in America," that they are recent fugitives from the six-day sock and saleratus Kultur of the cow and hog States. The artistic merchandise produced by liberated yokels of that sort is bound to show its intellectual newness, which is to say, its deficiency in civilized culture and sophistication. It is, on the plane of letters, precisely what evangelical Christianity is on the plane of religion, to wit, the product of ill-informed, emotional and more or less pushing and oafish folk. Life, to such Harvardized peasants, is not a mystery; it is something absurdly simple, to be described with surety and in a few words. 'If they set up as critics their criticism is all a matter of facile labeling, chiefly ethical; find the pigeon-hole, and the rest is easy. If they presume to discuss the great problems of human society, they are equally ready with their answers: draw up and pass a harsh enough statute, and the corruptible will straightway put on incorruption. And if, fanned by the soft breath of beauty, they go into practice as creative artists, as poets, as dramatists, as novelists, then one learns from them that we inhabit a country that is the model and despair of other states, that its culture is coextensive with human culture and enlightenment, and that every failure to find happiness under that culture is the result of sin.

6 Underlying Causes

Here is one of the fundamental defects of American fiction — perhaps the one character that sets it off sharply from all other known kinds of contemporary fiction. It habitually exhibits, not a man of delicate organization in revolt against the inexplicable tragedy of existence, but a man of low sensibilities and elemental desires yielding himself gladly to his environment, and so achieving what, under a third-rate civilization, passes for success. To get on: this is the aim. To weigh and reflect, to doubt and rebel: this is the thing to be avoided. I describe the optimistic, the inspirational, the Authors' League, the popular magazine, the peculiarly American school. In character creation its masterpiece is the advertising agent who, by devising some new and super-imbecile boobtrap, puts his hook-and-eye factory "on the map," ruins all other factories, marries the daughter of his boss, and so ends as an eminent man. Obviously, the drama underlying such fiction — what Mr. Beach would call its John Henry Plot — is false drama, Sunday-school drama, puerile and disgusting drama. It is the sort of thing that awakens a response only in men who are essentially unimaginative, timorous and degraded—in brief, in democrats, bagmen, yahoos. The man of reflective habit cannot conceivably take any passionate interest in the conflicts it deals with. He doesn't want to marry the daughter of the owner of the hook-and-eye factory; he would probably burn down the factory itself if it ever came into his hands. What interests this man is the far more poignant and significant conflict between a salient individual and the harsh and meaningless fiats of destiny, the unintelligible mandates and vagaries of God. His hero is not one who yields and wins, but one who resists and fails.

Most of these conflicts, of course, are internal, and hence do not make themselves visible in the overt melodrama of the Beaches, Davises and Chamberses. A superior man's struggle in the world is not with exterior lions, trusts, margraves, policemen, rivals in love, German spies, radicals and tornadoes, but with the obscure, atavistic impulses within him — the impulses, weaknesses and limitations that war with his notion of what life should be. Nine times out of ten he succumbs. Nine times out of ten he must yield to the dead hand. Nine times out of ten his aspiration is almost infinitely above his achievement. The result is that we see him sliding downhill — his ideals breaking up, his hope petering out, his character in decay. Character in decay is thus the theme of the great bulk of superior fiction. One has it in Dostoievsky, in Balzac, in Hardy, in Conrad, in Flaubert, in Zola, in Turgenieff, in Goethe, in Sudermann, in Bennett, and, to come home, in Dreiser. In nearly all first-rate novels the hero is defeated. In perhaps a majority he is completely destroyed. The hero of the inferior — i. e., the typically American — novel engages in no such doomed and fateful combat. His conflict is not with the inexplicable ukases of destiny, the limitations of his own strength, the dead hand upon him, but simply with the superficial desires of his elemental fellow men. He thus has a fair chance of winning — and in bad fiction that chance is always converted into a certainty. So he marries the daughter of the owner of the factory and eventually gobbles the factory itself. His success gives thrills to persons who can imagine no higher aspiration. He embodies their optimism, as the other hero embodies the pessimism of more introspective and idealistic men. He is the protagonist of that great majority which is so inferior that it is quite unconscious of its inferiority.

It is this superficiality of the inferior man, it seems to me, that is the chief hallmark of the American novel. Whenever one encounters a novel that rises superior to it the thing takes on a subtle but unmistakable air of foreignness— f or example, Frank Norris' "Vandover and the Brute," Hergesheimer's "The Lay Anthony" and Miss Gather's "My Antonia," or, to drop to short stories, Stephen Crane's "The Blue Hotel" and Mrs. Wharton's "Ethan Frome." The short story is commonly regarded, at least by American critics, as a preeminently American form; there are even patriots who argue that Bret Harte invented it. It meets very accurately, in fact, certain characteristic demands of the American temperament: it is simple, economical and brilliantly effective. Yet the same hollowness that marks the American novel also marks the American short story. Its great masters, in late years, have been such cheese-mongers as Davis, with his servant-girl romanticism, and o. Henry, with his smoke-room and variety show smartness. In the whole canon of o. Henry's work you will not find a single recognizable human character; his people are unanimously marionettes; he makes Mexican brigands, Texas cowmen and New York cracksmen talk the same highly ornate Broadwayese. The successive volumes of Edward J. "Brien's "Best Short-Story" series throw a vivid light upon the feeble estate of the art in the land. "Brien, though his aesthetic judgments are ludicrous, at least selects stories that are thoroughly representative; his books are trade successes because the crowd is undoubtedly with him. He has yet to discover a single story that even the most naive professor would venture to mention in the same breath with Joseph Conrad's "Heart of Darkness," or Andrieff's "Silence," or Sudermann's "Das Sterbelied," or the least considerable tale by Anatole France. In many of the current American makers of magazine short stories — for example, Gouverneur Morris — one observes, as I have said, a truly admirable technical skill. They have mastered the externals of the form. They know how to get their effects. But in content their work is as hollow as a jug. Such stuff has no imaginable relation to life as men live it in the world. It is as artificial as the heroic strut and romantic eyes of a moving-picture actor.

I have spoken of the air of foreignness that clings to certain exceptional American compositions. In part it is based upon a psychological trick — upon the surprise which must inevitably seize upon any one who encounters a decent piece of writing in so vast a desert of mere literacy. But in part it is grounded soundly enough on the facts. The native author of any genuine force and originality is almost invariably found to be under strong foreign influences, either English or Continental. It was so in the earliest days. Freneau, the poet of the Revolution, was thoroughly French in blood and traditions. Irving, as H. R. Haweis has said, "took to England as a duck takes to water," and was in exile seventeen years. Cooper, with the great success of "The Last of the Mohicans" behind him, left the country in disgust and was gone for seven years. Emerson, Bryant, Lowell, Hawthorne and even Longfellow kept their eyes turned across the water; Emerson, in fact, was little more than an importer and popularizer of German and French ideas. Bancroft studied in Germany; Prescott, like Irving, was enchanted by Spain. Poe, unable to follow the fashion, invented mythical travels to save his face — to France, to Germany, to the Greek isles. The Civil War revived the national consciousness enormously, but it did not halt the movement of emigres. Henry James, in the seventies, went to England, Bierce and Bret Harte followed him, and even Mark Twain, absolutely American though he was, was forever pulling up stakes and setting out for Vienna, Florence or London. Only poverty tied Whitman to the soil; his audience, for many years, was chiefly beyond the water, and there, too, he often longed to be. This distaste for the national scene is often based upon a genuine alienness. The more, indeed, one investigates the ancestry of Americans who have won distinction in the fine arts, the more one discovers tempting game for the critical Know Nothings. Whitman was half Dutch, Harte was half Jew, Poe was partly German, James had an Irish grandfather, Howells was largely Irish and German, Dreiser is German and Hergesheimer is Pennsylvania Dutch. Fully a half of the painters discussed in John C. van Dyke's "American Painting and Its Tradition" were of mixed blood, with the Anglo-Saxon plainly recessive. And of the five poets singled out for encomium by Miss Lowell in "Tendencies in Modern American Poetry" one is a Swede, two are partly German, one was educated in the German language, and three of the five exiled themselves to England as soon as they got out of their nonage. The exiles are of all sorts: Frank Harris, Vincent "Sullivan, Ezra Pound, Herman Scheffauer, T. S. Eliot, Henry B. Fuller, Stuart Merrill, Edith Wharton. They go to England, France, Germany, Italy — anywhere to escape. Even at home the literatus is perceptibly foreign in his mien. If he lies under the New England tradition he is furiously colonial — more English than the English. If he turns to revolt, he is apt to put on a French hat and a Russian red blouse. The Little Review, the organ of the extreme wing of revokes, is so violently exotic that several years ago, during the plupatriotic days of the war, some of its readers protested. With characteristic lack of humor it replied with an American number — and two of the stars of that number bore the fine old Anglo-Saxon names of Ben Hecht and Elsa von Freytag-Loringhoven.

This tendency of American literature, the moment it begins to show enterprise, novelty and significance, to radiate an alien smell is not an isolated phenomenon. The same smell accompanies practically all other sorts of intellectual activity in the republic. Whenever one hears that a new political theory is in circulation, or a scientific heresy, or a movement toward rationalism in religion, it is always safe to guess that some discontented stranger or other has a hand in it. In the newspapers and on the floor of Congress a new heterodoxy is always denounced forthwith as a product of foreign plotting, and here public opinion undoubtedly supports both the press and the politicians, and with good reason. The native culture of the country — that is, the culture of the low caste '"Anglo-Saxons who preserve the national tradition— is almost completely incapable of producing ideas. It is a culture that roughly corresponds to what the culture of England would be if there were no universities over there, and no caste of intellectual individualists and no landed aristocracy — in other words, if the tone of the national thinking were set by the nonconformist industrials, the camorra of Welsh and Scotch political scoundrels, and the town and country mobs. As we shall see, the United States has not yet produced anything properly describable as an aristocracy, and so there is no impediment to the domination of the inferior orders. Worse, the Anglo-Saxon strain, second-rate at the start, has tended to degenerate steadily to lower levels — in New England, very markedly. The result is that there is not only a great dearth of ideas in the land, but also an active and relentless hostility to ideas. The chronic suspiciousness of the inferior man here has full play; never in modern history has there been another civilization showing so vast a body of prohibitions and repressions, in both conduct and thought. The second result is that intellectual experimentation is chiefly left to the immigrants of the later migrations, and to the small sections of the native population that have been enriched with their blood. For such a pure Anglo-Saxon as Cabell to disport himself in the field of ideas is a rarity in the United States — and no exception to the rule that I have just mentioned, for Cabell belongs to an aristocracy that is now almost extinct, and has no more in common with the general population than a Baltic baron has with the indigenous herd of Letts and Esthonians. All the arts in America are thoroughly exotic. Music is almost wholly German or Italian, painting is French, literature may be anything from English to Russian, architecture (save when it becomes a mere branch of engineering) is a maddening phantasmagoria of borrowings. Even so elemental an art as that of cookery shows no native development, and is greatly disesteemed by Americans of the Anglo-Saxon majority; any decent restaurant that one blunders upon in the land is likely to be French, and if not French, then Italian or German or Chinese. So with the sciences: they have scarcely any native development. Organized scientific research began in the country with the founding of the Johns Hopkins University, a bald imitation of the German universities, and long held suspect by native opinion. Even after its great success, indeed, there was rancorous hostility to its scheme of things on chauvinistic grounds" and some years ago efforts were begun to Americanize it, with the result that it is now sunk to the level of Princeton, Amherst and other such glorified high-schools, and is dominated by native savants who would be laughed at in any Continental university. Science, oppressed by such assaults from below, moves out of the academic grove into the freer air of the great foundations, where the pursuit of the shy fact is uncontaminated by football and social pushing. The greatest of these foundations is the Rockefeller Institute. Its salient men are such investigators as Flexner, Loeb and Carrel — all of them Continental Jews.

Thus the battle of ideas in the United States is largely carried on under strange flags, and even the stray natives on the side of free inquiry have to sacrifice some of their nationality when they enlist. The effects of this curious condition of affairs are both good and evil. The good ones are easily apparent. The racial division gives the struggle a certain desperate earnestness, and even bitterness, and so makes it the more inviting to lively minds. It was a benefit to the late D. C. Gilman rather than a disadvantage that national opinion opposed his traffic with Huxley and the German professors in the early days of the Johns Hopkins; the stupidity of the opposition stimulated him, and made him resolute, and his resolution, in the long run, was of inestimable cultural value. Scientific research in America, indeed, was thus set securely upon its legs precisely because the great majority of right-thinking Americans were violently opposed to it. In the same way it must be obvious that Dreiser got something valuable out of the grotesque war that was carried on against him during the greater war overseas because of his German name — a jehad fundamentally responsible for the suppression of "The 'Genius' " The chief danger that he ran six or seven years ago was the danger that he might be accepted, explained away, and so seduced downward to the common level. The attack of professional patriots saved him from that calamity. More, it filled him with a keen sense of his isolation, and stirred up the vanity that was in him as it is in all of us, and so made him cling with new tenacity to the very peculiarities that differentiate him from his inferiors. Finally, it is not to be forgotten that, without this rebellion of immigrant iconoclasts, the whole body of the national literature would tend to sink to the 100% American level of such patriotic literary business men as the president of the Authors' League. In other words, we must put up with the esthetic Bolshevism of the Europeans and Asiatics who rage in the land, for without them we might not have any literature at all.

But the evils of the situation are not to be gainsaid. One of them I have already alluded to: the tendency of the beginning literatus, once he becomes fully conscious of his foreign affiliations, to desert the republic forthwith, and thereafter view it from afar, and as an actual foreigner. More solid and various cultures lure him; he finds himself uncomfortable at home. Sometimes, as in the case of Henry James, he becomes a downright expatriate, and a more or less active agent of anti- American feeling; more often, he goes over to the outlanders without yielding up his theoretical citizenship, as in the cases of Irving, Harris, Pound and "Sullivan. But all this, of course, works relatively light damage, for not many native authors are footloose enough to indulge in any such physical desertion of the soil. Of much more evil importance is the tendency of the cultural alienism that I have described to fortify the uncontaminated native in his bilious suspicion of all the arts, and particularly of all artists. The news that the latest poet to flutter the dovecotes is a Jew, or that the last novelist mauled by comstockery has a German or Scandinavian or Russian name, or that the critic newly taken in sacrilege is a partisan of Viennese farce or of the French moral code or of English literary theory — this news, among a people so ill-informed, so horribly we)l-trained in flight from bugaboos, and so savagely suspicious of the unfamiliar in ideas, has the inevitable effect of stirring up opposition that quickly ceases to be purely aesthetic objection, and so becomes increasingly difficult to combat. If Dreiser's name were Tompkins or Simpson, there is no doubt whatever that he would affright the professors a good deal less, and appear less of a hobgoblin to the *intelligentsia* of the women's clubs. If Oppenheim were less palpably levantine, he would come much nearer to the popularity of Edwin Markham and Walt Mason. And if Cabell kept to the patriotic business of a Southern gentleman, to wit, the praise of General Robert E. Lee, instead of prowling the strange and terrible fields of mediaeval Provenge, it is a safe wager that he would be sold openly over the counter instead of stealthily behind the door.

In a previous work I have discussed this tendency in America to estimate the artist in terms of his secular character. During the war, when all of the national defects in intelligence were enormously accentuated, it went to ludicrous lengths. There were then only authors who were vociferous patriots and thus geniuses, and authors who kept their dignity and were thus suspect and without virtue. By this gauge Chambers became the superior of Dreiser and Cabell, and Joyce Kilmer and Amy Lowell were set above Sandburg and Oppenheim. The test was even extended to foreigners: by it H. G. Wells took precedence of Shaw, and Blasco Ibanez became a greater artist than Romain Rolland. But the thing is not peculiar to war times; when peace is densest it is to be observed. The man of letters, pure and simple, is a rarity in America. Almost always he is something else — and that something else commonly determines his public eminence. Mark Twain, with only his books to recommend him, would probably have passed into obscurity in middle age; it was in the character of a public entertainer, not unrelated to Coxey, Dr. Mary Walker and Citizen George Francis Train, that he wooed and won his country. The official criticism of the land denied him any solid literary virtue to the day of his death, and even to-day the campus critics and their journalistic valets stand aghast before "The Mysterious Stranger" and "What is Man?" Emerson passed through almost the same experience. It was not as a man of letters that he was chiefly thought of in his time, but as the prophet of a new cult, half religious, half philosophical, and wholly unintelligible to nine-tenths of those who discussed it. The first author of a handbook of American literature to sweep away the codfish Moses and expose the literary artist was the Polish Jew, Leon Kellner, of Czemowitz. So with Whitman and Poe — both hobgoblins far more than artists. So, even, with Howells: it was as the exponent of a dying culture that he was venerated, not as the practitioner of an art. Few actually read his books. His celebrity, of course, was real enough, but it somehow differed materially from that of a pure man of letters — say Shelley, Conrad, Hauptmann, Hardy or Synge. That he was himself keenly aware of the national tendency to judge an artist in terms of the citizen was made plain at the time of the Gorky scandal, when he joined Clemens in an ignominious desertion of Gorky, scared out of his wits by the danger of being manhandled for a violation of the national pecksniffery. Howells also refused to sign the Dreiser Protest. The case of Frank Harris is one eloquently m point. Harris has written, among other books, perhaps the best biography ever done by an American, Yet his politics keep him in a sort of Coventry and the average American critic would no more think of praising him than of granting Treitschke any merit as an historian.

7. The Lonesome Artist

Thus falsely judged by standards that have no intelligible appositeness when applied to an artist, however accurately they may weigh a stockbroker or a Presbyterian elder, and forced to meet not only the hunkerous indifference of the dominant mob but also the bitter and disingenuous opposition of the classes to which he might look reasonably for understanding and support, the American author is forced into a sort of social and intellectual vacuum, and lives out his days, as Henry James said of Hawthorne, "'an alien everywhere, an aesthetic solitary."

The wonder is that, in the face of so metallic and unyielding a front, any genuine artists in letters come to the front at all. But they constantly emerge; the first gestures are always on show; the prodigal and gorgeous life of the country simply forces a sensitive minority to make some attempt at representation and interpretation, and out of many trying there often appears one who can. The phenomenon of Dreiser is not unique. He had his forerunners in Fuller and Frank Norris and he has his compagnons du voyage in Anderson, Charles G. Norris and more than one other. But the fact only throws up his curious isolation in a stronger light. It would be difficult to imagine an artist of his sober purpose and high accomplishment, in any civilized country, standing so neglected. The prevailing criticism, when it cannot dispose of him by denying that he exists — in the two chief handbooks of latter-day literature by professors he is not even mentioned! — seeks to dispose of him by arraying the shoddy fury of the mob against him. When he was under attack by the Comstocks, more than one American critic gave covert aid to the common enemy, and it was with difficulty that the weight of the Authors' League was held upon his side. More help for him, in fact, came from England, and quite voluntarily, than could be drummed up for him at home. No public sense of the menace that the attack offered to free speech and free art was visible; it would have made a nine-days' sensation for any layman of public influence to have gone to his rescue, as would have certainly happened in France, England or Germany. As for the newspaper-reading mob, it probably went unaware of the business altogether. When Arnold Bennett, landing in New York some time previously, told the reporters that Dreiser was the American he most desired to meet, the news was quite unintelligible to perhaps nine readers out of ten: they had no more heard of Dreiser than their fathers had heard of Whitman in 1875.

So with all the rest. I have mentioned Harris. It would be difficult to imagine Rolland meeting such a fate in France or Shaw in England as he has met in the United States. "Sullivan, during the war, came home with "A Good Girl" in his pocket. The book was republished here — and got vastly less notice than the latest piece of trade-goods by Kathleen Norris. Fuller, early in his career, gave it up as hopeless. Norris died vainly battling for the young Dreiser. An Abraham

Cahan goes unnoticed. Miss Gather, with four sound books behind her, lingers in the twilight of an esoteric reputation. Cabell, comstocked, is apprehended by his country only as a novelist to be bought by stealth and read in private. When Hugh Walpole came to America a year or two ago he favored the newspapers, like Bennett before him, with a piece of critical news that must have puzzled all readers save a very small minority. Discussing the living American novelists worth heeding, he nominated three — and of them only one was familiar to the general run of novel-buyers, or had ever been mentioned by a native critic of the apostolic succession. Only the poets of the land seem to attract the notice of the professors, and no doubt this is largely because most of the more salient of them — notably Miss Lowell and Lindsay — are primarily pressagents. Even so, the attention that they get is seldom serious. The only professor that I know of who has discussed the matter in precise terms holds that Alfred Noyes is the superior of all of them. Moreover, the present extraordinary interest in poetry stops short with a few poets, and one of its conspicuous phenomena is its lack of concern with the poets outside the movement, some of them unquestionably superior to any within.

Nor is this isolation of the artist in America new. The contemporary view of Poe and Whitman was almost precisely like the current view of Dreiser and Cabell. Both were neglected by the Brahmins of their time, and both were regarded hostilely by the great body of right-thinking citizens. Poe, indeed, was the victim of a furious attack by Rufus W. Griswold, the Hamilton Wright Mabie of the time, and it set the tone of native criticism for years. Whitman, living, narrowly escaped going to jail as a public nuisance. One thinks of Hawthorne and Emerson as writers decently appreciated by their contemporaries, but it is not to be forgotten that the official criticism of the era saw no essential difference between Hawthorne and Cooper, and that Emerson's reputation, to the end of his life, was far more that of a theological prophet and ethical platitudinarian, comparable to Lyman Abbott or Frank Crane, than that of a literary artist, comparable to Tennyson or Matthew Arnold. Perhaps Carlyle understood him, but who in America understood him? To this day he is the victim of gross misrepresentation by enthusiasts who read into him all sorts of flatulent bombast, as Puritanism is read into the New Testament by Methodists. As for Hawthorne, his extraordinary physical isolation during his lifetime was but the symbol of a complete isolation of the spirit, still surviving. If his preference for the internal conflict as opposed to the external act were not sufficient to set him off from the main stream of American speculation, there would always be his profound ethical skepticism — a state of mind quite impossible to the normal American, at least of Anglo-Saxon blood. Hawthorne, so far as I know, has never had a single professed follower in his own country. Even his son, attempting to carry on his craft, yielded neither to his meticulous method nor to his detached point of view. In the third generation, with infinite irony, there is a grand-daughter who is a reviewer of books for the New York Times, which is almost as if Wagner should have a grand-daughter singing in the operas of Massenet.

Of the four indubitable masters thus named, Hawthorne, Emerson, Whitman and Poe, only the last two have been sufficiently taken into the consciousness of the country to have any effect upon its literature, and even here that influence has been exerted only at second-hand, and against very definite adverse pressure. It would certainly seem reasonable for a man of so forceful a habit of mind as Poe, and of such prodigal and arresting originality, to have founded a school, but a glance at the record shows that he did nothing of the sort. Immediately he was dead, the shadows of the Irving tradition closed around his tomb, and for nearly thirty years thereafter all of his chief ideas went disregarded in his own country. If, as the literature books argue, Poe was the father of the American short story, then it was a posthumous child, and had step-fathers who did their best to conceal its true parentage. When it actually entered upon the vigorous life that we know to-day Poe had been dead for a generation. Its father, at the time of its belated adolescence, seemed to be Bret Harte — and Harte's debt to Dickens was vastly more apparent, first and last, than his debt to Poe. What he got from Poe was essential; it was the inner structure of the modern short story, the fundamental devices whereby a mere glimpse at events could be made to yield brilliant and seemingly complete images. But he himself was probably largely unaware of this indebtedness. A man little given to critical analysis, and incompetent for it when his own work was under examination, he saw its externals much more clearly than he saw its intrinsic organization, and these externals bore the plain marks of Dickens. It remained for one of his successors, Ambrose Bierce, to bridge belatedly the space separating him from Poe, and so show the route that he had come. And it remained for foreign criticism, and particularly for French criticism, to lift Poe himself to the secure place that he now holds. It is true enough that he enjoyed, during his lifetime, a certain popular reputation, and that he was praised by such men as N. P. Willis and James Russell Lowell, but that reputation was considerably less than the fame of men who were much his inferiors, and that praise, especially in Lowell's case, was much corrupted by reservations.

Not many native critics of respectable position, during the 50's and 60's, would have ranked him clearly above, say, Irving or Cooper, or even above Longfellow, his old enemy. A few partisans argued for him, but in the main, as Saintsbury has said, he was the victim of "extreme and almost incomprehensible injustice" at the hands of his countrymen. It is surely not without significance that it took ten years to raise money enough to put a cheap and hideous tombstone upon his neglected grave, that it was not actually set up until he had been dead twenty-six years, that no contemporary American writer took any part in furthering the project, and that the only one who attended the final ceremony was Whitman. It was Baudelaire's French translation of the prose tales and Mallarme's translation of the poems that brought Poe to Valhalla. The former, first printed in 1856, founded the Poe cult in France, and during the two decades following it flourished amazingly, and gradually extended to England and Germany. It was one of the well-springs, in fact, of the whole so-called decadent movement. If Baudelaire, the father of that movement, "cultivated hysteria with delight and terror," he was simply doing what Poe had done before him. Both, reacting against the false concept of beauty as a mere handmaiden of logical ideas, 'nought its springs in those deep feelings and inner experiences which lie beyond the range of ideas and are to be interpreted only as intuitions. Emerson started upon the same quest, but was turned off into mazes of contradiction and unintelligibility by his ethical obsession — the unescapable burden of his Puritan heritage.

But Poe never wandered from the path. You will find in "The Poetic Principle" what is perhaps the clearest statement of this new and sounder concept of beauty that has ever been made — certainly it is clearer than any ever made by a Frenchman. But it was not until Frenchmen had watered the seed out of grotesque and van-colored pots that it began to sprout. The tide of Poe's ideas, set in motion in France early in the second half of the century, did not wash England until the last decade, and in America, save for a few dashes of spray, it has yet to show itself. There is no American writer who displays the influence of this most potent and original of Americans so clearly as whole groups of Frenchmen display it, and whole groups of Germans, and even a good many Englishmen. What we have from Poe at first hand is simply a body of obvious yokel-shocking in the Black Cat manner, with the tales of Ambrose Bierce as its finest flower — in brief, an imitation of Poe's externals without any comprehension whatever of his underlying aims and notions. What we have from him at second-hand is a somewhat childish Maeterlinckism, a further dilution of Poe-and-water. This Maeterlinckism, some time ago, got itself intermingled with the Whitmanic stream flowing back to America through the channel of French Imagism, with results destructive to the sanity of earnest critics and fatal to the gravity of those less austere. It is significant that the critical writing of Poe, in which there lies most that was best in him, has not come back; no normal American ever thinks of him as a critic, but only as a poet, as a raiser of goose-flesh, or as an immoral fellow. The cause thereof is plain enough. The French, instead of borrowing his critical theory directly, deduced it afresh from his applications of it; it became criticism of him rather than by him. Thus his own speculations have lacked the authority of foreign approval, and have consequently made no impression. The weight of native opinion is naturally against them, for they are at odds, not only with its fundamental theories, but also with its practical doctrine that no criticism can be profound and respectable which is not also dull.

'Poe" says Arthur Ransome, in his capital study of the man and the artist, 'was like a wolf chained by the leg among a lot of domestic dogs." The simile here is somewhat startling, and Ransome, in a footnote, tries to ameliorate it: the "domestic dogs" it refers to were magnificoes of no less bulk than Longfellow, Whittier, Holmes and Emerson. In the case of Whitman, the wolf was not only chained, but also muzzled. Nothing, indeed, could be more amazing than the hostility that surrounded him at home until the very end of his long life. True enough, it was broken by certain feeble mitigations. Emerson, in 1855, praised him — though later very eager to forget it and desert him, as

Clemens and Howells, years afterward, deserted Gorky. Alcott, Thoreau, Lowell and even Bryant, during his brief Bohemian days.

were polite to him. A group of miscellaneous enthusiasts gradually gathered about him, and out of this group emerged at least one man of some distinction, John Burroughs. Young adventurers of letters — for example, Huneker — went to see him and hear him, half drawn by genuine admiration and half by mere deviltry. But the general tone of the opinion that beat upon him, the attitude of domestic criticism, was unbrokenly inimical; he was opposed by misrepresentation and neglect. "The prevailing range of criticism on my book," he wrote in "A Backward Glance on My Own Road" in 1884, "has been either mockery or denunciation — and . . • I have been the marked object of two or three (to me pretty serious) official buffetings." "After thirty years of trial," he wrote in "My Book and I," three years later, "public criticism on the book and myself as author of it shows marked anger and contempt more than anything else." That is, at home. Abroad he was making headway all the while, and long years afterward, by way of France and England, he began to force his way into the consciousness of his countrymen. What could have been more ironical than the solemn celebrations of Whitman's centenary that were carried off in various American universities in 1919? One can picture the old boy rolling with homeric mirth in hell. Imagine the fate of a university don of 1860, or 1870, or 1880, or even 1890 who had ventured to commend "Leaves of Grass" to the young gentlemen of his seminary! He would have come to grief as swiftly as that Detroit pedagogue of day before yesterday who brought down the Mothers' Legion upon him by commending "Jurgen."

8. The Cultural Background

So far, the disease. As to the cause, I have delivered a few hints. I now describe it particularly. It is, in brief, a defect in the general culture of the country — one reflected, not only in the national literature, but also in the national political theory, the national attitude toward religion and morals, the national habit in all departments of thinking. It is the lack of a civilized aristocracy, secure in its position, animated by an intelligent curiosity, skeptical of all facile generalizations, superior to the sentimentality of the mob, and delighting in the battle of ideas for its own sake.

The word I use, despite the qualifying adjective, has got itself meanings, of course, that I by no means intend to convey. Any mention of an aristocracy, to a public fed upon democratic fustian, is bound to bring up images of stockbrokers' wives lolling obscenely in opera boxes, or of haughty Englishmen slaughtering whole generations of grouse in an inordinate and incomprehensible manner, or of Junkers with tight waists elbowing American schoolmarms off the sidewalks of German beer towns, or of perfumed Italians coming over to work their abominable magic upon the daughters of breakfast-food and bathtub kings. Part of this misconception, I suppose, has its roots in the gaudy imbecilities of the yellow press, but there is also a part that belongs to the general American tradition, along with the oppression of minorities and the belief in political panaceas. Its depth and extent are constantly revealed by the naive assumption that the so-called fashionable folk of the large cities — chiefly wealthy industrials in the interior-decorator and country-club stage of culture — constitute an aristocracy, and by the scarcely less remarkable assumption that the peerage of England is identical with the gentry — that is, that such men as Lord Northcliffe, Lord Iveagh and even Lord Reading are English gentlemen, and of the ancient line of the Percys.

Here, as always, the worshiper is the father of the gods, and no less when they are evil than when they are benign. The inferior man must find himself superiors, that he may marvel at his political equality with them, and in the absence of recognizable superiors de facto he creates superiors de jure. The sublime principle of one man, one vote must be translated into terms of dollars, diamonds, fashionable intelligence; the equality of all men before the law must have clear and dramatic proofs. Sometimes, perhaps, the thing goes further and is more subtle. The inferior man needs an aristocracy to demonstrate, not only his mere equality, but also his actual superiority. The society columns in the newspapers may have some such origin: they may visualize once more the accomplished journalist's understanding of the mob mind that he plays upon so skillfully, as upon some immense and cacophonous organ, always going fortissimo. What the inferior man and his wife see in the sinister revels of those amazing first families, I suspect, is often a massive witness to their own higher rectitude — to their relative innocence of cigarette-smoking, poodle-coddling, child-farming and the more abstruse branches of adultery — in brief, to their firmer grasp upon the immutable axioms of Christian virtue, the one sound boast of the nether nine-tenths of humanity in every land under the cross.

But this bugaboo aristocracy, as I hint, is actually bogus, and the evidence of its bogusness lies in the fact that it is insecure. One gets into it only onerously, but out of it very easily. Entrance is effected by dint of a long and bitter struggle, and the chief incidents of that struggle are almost intolerable humiliations. The aspirant must school and steel himself to sniffs and sneers; he must see the door slammed upon him a hundred times before ever it is thrown open to him. To get in at all he most show a talent for abasement — and abasement makes him timorous. Worse, that timorousness is not cored when he succeeds at last. On the contrary, it is made even more tremulous, for what he faces within the gates is a scheme of things made up almost wholly of harsh and often unintelligible taboos, and the penalty for violating even the least of them is swift and disastrous. He must exhibit exactly the right social habits, appetites and prejudices, public and private. He must harbor exactly the right political enthusiasms and indignations. He must have a hearty taste for exactly the right sports. His attitude toward the fine arts must be properly tolerant and yet not a shade too eager. He must read and like exactly the right books, pamphlets and public journals. He must put up at the right hotels when he travels. His wife must patronize the right milliners. He himself must stick to the right haberdashery. He must live in the right neighborhood. He must even embrace the right doctrines of religion. It would ruin him, for all opera box and society column purposes, to set up a plea for justice to the Bolsheviki, or even for ordinary decency. It would ruin him equally to wear celluloid collars, or to move to Union Hill, N. J., or to serve ham and cabbage at his table. And it would ruin him, too, to drink coffee from his saucer, or to marry a chambermaid with a gold tooth, or to join the Seventh Day Adventists. Within the boundaries of his curious order he is worse fettered than a monk in a cell. Its obscure conception of propriety, its nebulous notion that this or that is honorable, hampers him in every direction, and very narrowly. What he resigns when he enters, even when he makes his first deprecating knock at the door, is every right to attack the ideas that happen to prevail within. Such as they are, he must accept them without question. And as they shift and change in response to great instinctive movements (or perhaps, now and then, to the punished but not to be forgotten revolts of extraordinary rebels) he must shift and change with them, silently and quickly. To hang back, to challenge and dispute, to preach reforms and revolutions — these are crimes against the brummagen Holy Ghost of the order.

Obviously, that order cannot constitute a genuine aristocracy, in any rational sense. A genuine aristocracy is grounded upon very much different principles. Its first and most salient character is its interior security, and the chief visible evidence of that security is the freedom that goes with it — not only freedom in act, the divine right of the aristocrat to do what he jolly well pleases, so long as he does not violate the primary guarantees and obligations of his class, but also and more importantly freedom in thought, the liberty to try and err, the right to be his own man. It is the instinct of a true aristocracy, not to punish eccentricity by expulsion, but to throw a mantle of protection about it— to safeguard it from the suspicions and resentments of the lower orders. Those lower orders are inert, timid, inhospitable to ideas, hostile to changes, faithful to a few maudlin superstitions. All progress goes on on the higher levels. It is there that salient personalities, made secure by artificial immunities, may oscillate most widely from the normal track. It is within that entrenched fold, out of reach of the immemorial certainties of the mob, that extraordinary men of the lower orders may find their city of refuge, and breathe a clear air. This, indeed, is at once the hall-mark and the justification of an aristocracy — that it is beyond responsibility to the general masses of men, and hence superior to both their degraded longings and their no less degraded aversions. It is nothing if it is not autonomous, curious, venturesome, courageous, and everything if it is. It is the custodian of the qualities that make for change and experiment; it is the class that organizes danger to the service of the race; it pays for its high prerogatives by standing in the forefront of the fray.

No such aristocracy, it must be plain, is now on view in the United States. The makings of one were visible in the Virginia of the later eighteenth century, but with Jefferson and Washington the promise died. In New England, it seems to me, there was never any aristocracy, either in being or in nascency: there was only a theocracy that degenerated very quickly into a plutocracy on the one hand and a caste of sterile Gelekrten on the other — the passion for God splitting into a lust for dollars and a weakness for mere words. Despite the common notion to the contrary — a notion generated by confusing literacy with intelligence — New England has never shown the slightest sign of a genuine enthusiasm for ideas. It began its history as a slaughter-house of ideas, and it is to-day not easily distinguishable from a cold-storage plant. Its celebrated adventures in mysticism, once apparently so bold and significant, are now seen to have been little more than an elaborate hocus-pocus — respectable Unitarians shocking the peasantry and scaring the homed cattle in the fields by masquerading in the robes of Roscicrucians. The ideas that it embraced in those austere and far-off days were stale, and when it had finished with them they were dead: to-day one hears of Jakob Bohme almost as rarely as one hears of Allen G. Thurman. So in politics. Its glory is Abolition— an English invention, long under the interdict of the native plutocracy. Since the Civil War its six states have produced fewer political ideas, as political ideas run in the Republic, than any average county in Kansas or Nebraska. Appomattox seemed to be a victory for New England idealism. It was actually a victory for the New England plutocracy, and that plutocracy has dominated thou" above the Housatonic ever since. The sect of professional idealists has so far dwindled that it has ceased to be of any importance, even as an opposition. When the plutocracy is challenged now, it is challenged by the proletariat.

Well, what is on view in New England is on view in all other parts of the nation, sometimes with ameliorations, but usually with the colors merely exaggerated. What one beholds, sweeping the eye over the land, is a culture that, like the national literature, is in three layers — the plutocracy on top, a vast mass of undifferentiated human blanks at the bottom, and a forlorn intelligentsia gasping out a precarious life between. I need not set out at any length, I hope, the intellectual deficiencies of the plutocracy — its utter failure to show anything even remotely resembling the makings of an aristocracy. It is badly educated, it is stupid, it is full of low-caste superstitions and indignations, it is without decent traditions or informing vision; above all, it is extraordinarily lacking in the most elemental independence and courage. Out of this class comes the grotesque fashionable society of our big towns, already described. Imagine a horde of peasants incredibly enriched and with almost infinite power thrust into their hands, and you will have a fair picture of its habitual state of mind.

It shows all the stigmata of inferiority — moral certainty, cruelty, suspicion of ideas, fear. Never did it function more revealingly than in the late pogrom against the so-called Reds, i. e., against humorless idealists who, like Andrew Jackson, took the platitudes of democracy quite seriously. The machinery brought to bear upon these feeble and scattered fanatics would have almost sufficed to repel an invasion by the united powers of Europe. They were hunted out of their sweat-shops and coffee-houses as if they were so many Carranzas or Ludendorffs, dragged to jail to the tooting of horns, arraigned before quaking judges on unintelligible charges, condemned to deportation without the slightest chance to defend them: selves, torn from their dependent families, herded into prison-ships, and then finally dumped in a snow waste, to be rescued and fed by the Bolsheviki. And what was the theory at the bottom of all these astounding proceedings? So far as it can be reduced to comprehensible terms it was much less a theory than a fear — a shivering, idiotic, discreditable fear of a mere banshee — an overpowering, paralyzing dread that some extra-eloquent Red, permitted to emit his balderdash unwhipped, might eventually convert a couple of courageous men, and that the courageous men, filled with indignation against the plutocracy, might take to the highroad, burn down a nail-factory or two, and slit the throat of some virtuous profiteer.

In order to lay this fear, in order to ease the jangled nerves of the American successors to the Hapsburgs and Hohenzollems, all the constitutional guarantees of the citizen were suspended, the statute-books were burdened with laws that surpass anything heard of in the Austria of Maria Theresa, the country was handed over to a frenzied mob of detectives, informers and agents provocateurs — and the Reds departed laughing loudly, and were hailed by the Bolsheviki as innocents escaped from an asylum for the criminally insane.

Obviously, it is out of reason to look for any hospitality to ideas in a class so extravagantly fearful of even the most palpably absurd of them. Its philosophy is firmly grounded upon the thesis that the existing order must stand forever free from attack, and not only from attack, but also from mere academic criticism, and its ethics are as firmly grounded upon the thesis that every attempt at any such criticism is a proof of moral turpitude. Within its own ranks, protected by what may be regarded as the privilege of the order, there is nothing to take the place of this criticism. A few feeble platitudes by Andrew Carnegie and a book of moderate merit by John D. Rockefeller's press-agent constitute almost the whole of the interior literature of ideas. In other countries the plutocracy has often produced men of reflective and analytical habit, eager to rationalize its instincts and to bring it into some sort of relationship to the main streams of human thought. The case of David Ricardo at once comes to mind. There have been many others: John Bright, Richard Gibden, George Grote, and, in our own time, Walther von Rathenau. But in the United States no such phenomenon has been visible. There was a day, not long ago, when certain young men of wealth gave signs of an unaccustomed interest in ideas on the political side, but the most they managed to achieve was a banal sort of Socialism, and even this was abandoned in sudden terror when the war came, and Socialism fell under suspicion of being genuinely international — in brief, of being honest under the skin. Nor has the plutocracy of the country ever fostered an inquiring spirit among its intellectual valets and footmen, which is to say, among the gentlemen who compose headlines and leading articles for its newspapers. What chiefly distinguishes the daily press of the United States from the press of all other countries pretending to culture is not its lack of truthfulness or even its lack of dignity and honor, for these deficiencies are common to the newspapers everywhere, but its incurable fear of ideas, its constant effort to evade the discussion of fundamentals by translating all issues into a few elemental fears, its incessant reduction of all reflection to mere emotion. It is, in the true sense, never well-informed. It is seldom intelligent, save in the arts of the mob-master. It is never courageously honest. Held harshly to a rigid correctness of opinion by the plutocracy that controls it with less and less attempt at disguise, and menaced on all sides by censorships that it dare not flout, it sinks rapidly into formalism and feebleness. Its yellow section is perhaps its most respectable section, for there the only vestige of the old free journalist survives. In the more conservative papers one finds only a timid and petulant animosity to all questioning of the existing order, however urbane and sincere— a pervasive and ill-concealed dread that the mob now heated up against the orthodox hobgoblins may suddenly begin to unearth hobgoblins of its own, and so run amok. For it is upon the emotions of the mob, of course, that the whole comedy is played. Theoretically the mob is the repository of all political wisdom and virtue; actually it is the ultimate source of all political power. Even the plutocracy cannot make war upon it openly, or forget the least of its weaknesses. The business of keeping it in order must be done discreetly, warily, with delicate technique. In the main that business consists of keeping alive its deep-seated fears — of strange faces, of unfamiliar ideas, of unhackneyed gestures, of untested liberties and responsibilities. The one permanent emotion of the inferior man, as of all the simpler mammals, is fear — fear of the unknown, the complex, the inexplicable. What he wants beyond everything else is safety. His instincts incline him toward a society so organized that it will protect him at all hazards, and not only against perils to his hide but also against assaults upon his mind — against the need to grapple with unaccustomed problems, to weigh ideas, to think things out for himself, to scrutinize the platitudes upon which his everyday thinking is based. Content under kaiserism so long as it functions efficiently, he turns, when kaiserism falls, to some other and perhaps worse form of paternalism, bringing to its benign tyranny only the docile tribute of his pathetic allegiance. In America it is the newspaper that is his boss. From it he gets support for his elemental illusions. In it he sees a visible embodiment of his own wisdom and consequence. Out of it he draws fuel for his simple moral passion, his congenital suspicion of heresy, his dread of the unknown. And behind the newspaper stands the plutocracy, ignorant, unimaginative and timorous.

Thus at the top and at the bottom. Obviously, there is no aristocracy here. One finds only one of the necessary elements, and that only in the plutocracy, to wit, a truculent egoism. But where is intelligence? Where are ease and surety of manner? Where are enterprise and curiosity? Where, above all, is courage, and in particular, moral courage — the capacity for independent thinking, for difficult problems, for what Nietzsche called the joys of the labyrinth? As well look for these things in a society of half-wits. Democracy, obliterating the old aristocracy, has left only a vacuum in its place; in a century and a half it has failed either to lift up the mob to intellectual autonomy and dignity or to purge the plutocracy of its inherent stupidity and swinishness. It is precisely here, the first and favorite scene of the Great Experiment, that the culture of the individual has been reduced to the most rigid and absurd regimentation. It is precisely here, of all civilized countries, that eccentricity in demeanor and opinion has come to bear the heaviest penalties" The whole drift of our law is toward the absolute prohibition of all ideas that diverge in the slightest from the accepted platitudes, and behind that drift of law there is a far more potent force of growing custom, and under that custom there is a national philosophy which erects conformity into the noblest of virtues and the free functioning of personality into a capital crime against society.

9. Under the Campus Pump

But there remain the intelligentsia, the free spirits in the middle ground, neither as anaesthetic to ideas as the plutocracy on the one hand nor as much the slaves of emotion as the proletariat on the other. Have I forgotten them? I have not. But what actually reveals itself when this small brotherhood of the superior is carefully examined? What reveals itself, it seems to me, is a gigantic disappointment. Superficially, there are all the marks of a caste of learned and sagacious men — a great book-knowledge, a laudable diligence, a certain fine reserve and sniffishness, a plain consciousness of intellectual superiority, not a few gestures that suggest the aristocratic. But under the surface one quickly discovers that the whole thing is little more than play-acting, and not always very skillful. Learning is there, but not curiosity. A heavy dignity is there, but not much genuine self-respect. Pretentiousness is there, but not a trace of courage. Squeezed between the plutocracy on on side and the mob on the other, the intelligentsia face the eternal national problem of maintaining their position, of guarding themselves against challenge and attack, of keeping down suspicion. They have all the attributes of knowledge save the sense of power. They have all the qualities of an aristocracy save the capital qualities that arise out of a feeling of security, of complete independence, of absolute immunity to onslaught from above and below. In brief, the old bogusness hangs about them, as about the fashionable aristocrats of the society columns. They are safe so long as they are good, which is to say, so long as they neither aggrieve the plutocracy nor startle the proletariat. Immediately they fall into either misdemeanor all their apparent dignity vanishes, and with it all of their influence, and they become simply somewhat ridiculous rebels against a social order that has no genuine need of them and is disposed to tolerate them only when they are not obtrusive.

For various reasons this shadowy caste is largely made up of men who have official stamps upon their learning — that is, of professors, of doctors of philosophy; outside of academic circles it tends to shade off very rapidly into a half-world of isolated anarchists. One of those reasons is plain enough: the old democratic veneration for mere schooling, inherited from the Puritans of New England, is still in being, and the mob, always eager for short cuts in thinking, is disposed to accept a schoolmaster without looking beyond his degree. Another reason lies in the fact that the higher education is still rather a novelty in the country, and there have yet to be developed any devices for utilizing learned men in any trade save teaching. Yet other reasons will suggest themselves. Whatever the ramification of causes, the fact is plain that the pedagogues have almost a monopoly of what passes for the higher thinking in the land. Not only do they reign unchallenged in their own chaste grove; they also penetrate to all other fields of ratiocination, to the almost complete exclusion of unshrived rivals. They dominate the weeklies of opinion; they are to the fore in every review; they write nine-tenths of the serious books of the country; they begin to invade the newspapers; they instruct and exhort the yokelry from the stump; they have even begun to penetrate into the government. One cannot turn in the United States without encountering a professor. There is one on every municipal commission. There is one in every bureau of the federal government. There is one at the head of every intellectual movement. There is one to explain every new mystery. Professors appraise all works of art, whether graphic, tonal or literary. Professors supply the brain power for agriculture, diplomacy, the control of dependencies and the distribution of commodities. A professor was until lately sovereign of the country, and pope of the state church.

So much for their opportunity. What, now, of their achievement? I answer as one who has had thrown upon him, by the impenetrable operations of fate, the rather thankless duties of a specialist in the ways of pedagogues, a sort of professor of professors. The job has got me enemies. I have been accused of carrying on a defamatory jehad against virtuous and laborious men; I have even been charged with doing it in the interest of the Wilhelmstrasse, the White Slave Trust and the ghost of Friedrich Wilhelm Nietzsche. Nothing could be more absurd. All my instincts are on the side of the professors. I

esteem a man who devotes himself to a subject with hard diligence; I esteem even more a man who puts poverty and a shelf of books above profiteering and evenings of jazz; I am naturally monkish. More' over, there are more Ph.D.'s on my family tree than even a Boston bluestocking can boast; there was a whole century when even the most ignorant of my house was at least Juris utriusque Doctor. But such predispositions should not be permitted to color sober researches. What I have found, after long and arduous labors, is a state of things that is surely not altogether flattering to the Gelehrten under examination. What I have found, in brief, is that pedagogy turned to general public uses is almost as timid and flatulent as journalism — that the professor, menaced by the timid dogmatism of the plutocracy above him and the incurable suspiciousness of the mob beneath him, is almost invariably inclined to seek his own security in a mellifluous inanity — that, far from being a courageous spokesman of ideas and an apostle of their free dissemination, in politics, in the fine arts, in practical ethics, he comes close to being the most prudent and skittish of all men concerned with them — in brief, that he yields to the prevailing correctness of thought in all departments, north, east, south and west, and is, in fact, the chief exponent among us of the democratic doctrine that heresy is not only a mistake, but also a crime.

A philosophy is not put to much of a test in ordinary times, for in ordinary times philosophies are permitted to lie like sleeping dogs. When it shows its inward metal is when the band begins to play. The turmoils of the late lamentable war, it seems to me, provided for such a trying out of fundamental ideas and attitudes upon a colossal scale. The whole thinking of the world was thrown into confusion; all the worst fears and prejudices of ignorant and emotional men came to the front; it was a time, beyond all others in modern history, when intellectual integrity was subjected to a cruel strain. How did the intelligentsia of These States bear up under that strain? What was the reaction of our learned men to the challenge of organized hysteria, mob fear, incitement to excess, downright insanity? How did they conduct themselves in that universal whirlwind? They conducted themselves, I fear, in a manner that must leave a brilliant question mark behind their claim to independence and courage, to true knowledge and dignity, to ordinary self-respect— in brief, to every quality that belongs to the authentic aristocrat. They constituted themselves, not a restraining influence upon the mob run wild, but the loudest spokesmen of its worst imbecilities. They fed it with bogus history, bogus philosophy, bogus idealism, bogus heroics. They manufactured blather for its entertainment. They showed themselves to be as naive as so many Liberty Loan orators, as emotional, almost, as the spy limiters, and as disdainful of the ordinary intellectual decencies as the editorial writers. I accumulated, in those great days, for the instruction and horror of posterity, a very large collection of academic arguments, expositions and pronunciamentos; it fills a trunk, and got me heavily into debt to three clipping-bureaux. Its contents range from solemn hymns of hate in the learned (and even the theological) reviews and such official donkeyisms as the formal ratification of the so-called Sisson documents down to childish harangues to student-bodies, public demands that the study of the enemy language and literature be prohibited by law, violent denunciations of all enemy science as negligible and fraudulent, vitriolic attacks upon enemy magnificos, and elaborate proofs that the American Revolution was the result of a foul plot hatched in the Wilhelmstrasse of the time, to the wanton injury of two loving bands of brothers. I do not exaggerate in the slightest. The proceedings of Mr. Creel's amazing corps of "twenty-five hundred American historians" went further than anything I have described. And in every far-flung college town, in every one-building "university" on the prairie, even the worst efforts of those "historians" were vastly exceeded.

But I am forgetting the like phenomena on the other side of the bloody chasm? I am overlooking the darker crimes of the celebrated German professors? Not at all. Those crimes against all reason and dignity, had they been committed in fact, would not be evidence in favor of the Americans in the dock: the principle of law is too well accepted to need argument. But I venture to deny them, and out of a very special and singular knowledge, for I seem to be one of the few Americans who has ever actually read the proclamations of the German professors: all the most indignant critics of them appear to have accepted second-hand accounts of their contents. Having suffered the onerous labor of reading them, I now offer sworn witness to their relative mildness. Now and then one encounters in them a disconcerting bray. Now and then one weeps with sore heart. Now and then one is bogged in German made wholly unintelligible by emotion. But taking them as they stand, and putting them fairly beside the corresponding documents of American vintage, one is at once struck by their comparative suavity and decorum, their freedom from mere rhetoric and fustian — above all, by their effort to appeal to reason, such as it is, rather than to emotion. No German professor, from end to end of the war, put his hand to anything as transparently silly as the Sisson documents. No German professor essayed to prove that the Seven Years' War was caused by Downing Street. No German professor argued that the study of English would corrupt the soul. No German professor denounced Darwin as an ignoramus and Lister as a scoundrel. Nor was anything of the sort done, so far as I know, by any French professor. Nor even by any reputable English professor. All such honor- able efforts on behalf of correct thought in war-time were monopolized by American professors. And if the fact is disputed, then I threaten upon some future day, when the stealthy yearning to forget has arisen, to print my proofs in parallel columns—the most esteemed extravagances of the German professors in one column and the corresponding masterpieces of the American professors in the other. I do not overlook, of course, the self-respecting men who, in the midst of all the uproar, kept their counsel and their dignity. A small minority, hard beset and tested by the fire! Nor do I overlook the few sentimental fanatics who, in the face of devastating evidence to the contrary, proceeded upon the assumption that academic freedom was yet inviolable, and so got themselves cashiered, and began posturing in radical circles as martyrs, the most absurd of men. But I think I draw a fair picture of the general. I think I depict with reasonable accuracy the typical response of the only recognizable intelligentsia of the land to the first great challenge to their aristocratic aloofness—the first test in the grand manner of their freedom alike from the bellicose imbecility of the plutocracy and the intolerable fears and childish moral certainties of the mob. That test exposed them shamelessly. It revealed their fast allegiance to the one thing that is the antithesis of all free inquiry, of all honest hospitality to ideas, of all intellectual independence and integrity. They proved that they were correct — and in proving it they threw a brilliant light upon many mysteries of our national culture.

10. The Intolerable Burden

Among others, upon the mystery of our literature — its faltering feebleness, its lack of genuine gusto, its dearth of salient personalities, its general air of poverty and imitation. What ails the beautiful letters of the Republic, I repeat, is what ails the general culture of the Republic — the lack of a body of sophisticated and civilized public opinion, independent of plutocratic control and superior to the infantile philosophies of the mob— a body of opinion showing the eager curiosity, the educated skepticism and the hospitality to ideas of a true aristocracy. This lack is felt by the American author, imagining him to have anything new to say, every day of his life. He can hope for no support, in ordinary cases, from the mob: it is too suspicious of all ideas. He can hope for no support from the spokesmen of the plutocracy: they are too diligently devoted to maintaining the intellectual status quo. He turns, then, to the intelligentsia—and what he finds is correctness! In his two prime functions, to represent the life about him accurately and to criticize it honestly, he sees that correctness arrayed against him. His representation is indecorous, unlovely, too harsh to be borne. His criticism is in contumacy to the ideals upon which the whole structure rests. So he is either attacked vigorously as an anti-patriot whose babblings ought to be put down by law, or enshrouded in a silence which commonly disposes of him even more effectively.

Soon or late, of course, a man of genuine force and originality is bound to prevail against that sort of stupidity. He will unearth an adherent here and another there; in the long run they may become numerous enough to force some recognition of him, even from the most immovable exponents of correctness. But the business is slow, uncertain, heart-breaking. It puts a burden upon the artist that ought not to be put upon him. It strains beyond reason his diligence and passion. A man who devotes his life to creating works of the imagination, a man who gives over all his strength and energy to struggling with problems that are essentially delicate and baffling and pregnant with doubt — such a man does not ask for recognition as a mere reward for his industry; he asks for it as a necessary help to his industry; he needs it as he needs decent subsistence and peace of mind. It is a grave damage to the artist and a grave loss to the literature when such a man as Poe has to seek consolation among his inferiors, and such a man as the Mark Twain of "What Is Man?" is forced to conceal his most profound beliefs, and such men as Dreiser and Cabell are exposed to incessant attacks by malignant stupidity. The notion that artists flourish upon adversity and misunderstanding, that they are able to function to the utmost in an atmosphere of indifference or hostility — this notion is nine-tenths nonsense. If it were true, then one would never hear of painters going to France or of musicians going to Germany. What the artist actually needs is comprehension of his aims and ideals by men he respects — not necessarily approval of his products, but simply an intelligent sympathy for him in the great agony of creation. And that sympathy must be more than the mere fellow-feeling of other craftsmen; it must come, in large part, out of a connoisseurship that is beyond the bald trade interest; it must have its roots in the intellectual curiosity of an aristocracy of taste. Billroth, I believe, was more valuable to Brahms than even Schumann. His eager interest gave music-making a solid dignity. His championship offered the musician a visible proof that his labors had got for him a secure place in a civilized and stable society, and that he would be judged by his peers, and safeguarded against the obtuse hostility of his inferiors.

No such security is thrown about an artist in America. It is not that the country lacks the standards that Dr. Brownell pleads for; it is that its standards are still those of a primitive and timorous society. The excesses of Comstockery are profoundly symbolical. What they show is the moral certainty of the mob in operation against something that is as incomprehensible to it as the theory of least squares, and what they show even more vividly is the distressing lack of any automatic corrective of that outrage — of any firm and secure body of educated opinion, eager to hear and test all intelligible ideas and sensitively jealous of the right to discuss them freely. When "The Genius" was attacked by the Comstocks, it fell to my lot to seek assistance for Dreiser among the intelligentsia. I found them almost unanimously disinclined to lend a hand. A small number permitted themselves to be induced, but the majority held back, and not a few, as I have said, actually offered more or less furtive aid to the Comstocks. I pressed the matter and began to unearth reasons. It was, it appeared, dangerous for a member of the intelligentsia" and particularly for a member of the academic intelligentsia, to array himself against the mob inflamed — against the moral indignation of the sort of folk who devour vice reports and are converted by the Rev. Billy Sunday! If he came forward, he would have to come forward alone. There was no organized support behind him. No instinctive urge of class, no prompting of a great tradition, moved him to speak out for artistic freedom . England supplied the lack. Over there they have a mob too, and something akin to Comstockery, and a cult of hollow correctness — but they also have a caste that stands above all that sort of thing, and out of that caste came aid for Dreiser.

England is always supplying the lack — England, or France, or Germany, or some other country, but chiefly England. "My market and my reputation," said Prescott in 1838, "rest principally with England." To Poe, a few years later, the United States was "a literary colony of Great Britain." And there has been little change to this day. The English leisure class, says Prof. Dr. Veblen, is "for purposes of reputable usage the upper leisure class of this country." Despite all the current highfalutin about melting pots and national destinies the United States remains almost as much an English colonial possession, intellectually and spiritually, as it was on July 3, 1776. The American social pusher keeps his eye on Mayfair; the American literatus dreams of recognition by the London weeklies; the American don is lifted to bliss by the imprimatur of Oxford or Cambridge; even the American statesman knows how to cringe to Downing Street. Most of the essential policies of Dr. Wilson between 1914 and 1920 — when the realistic English, finding him no longer useful, incontinently dismissed him — were, to all intents and purposes, those of a British colonial premier. He went into the Peace Conference willing to yield everything to English interests, and he came home with a treaty that was so extravagantly English that it fell an easy prey to the anti-English minority, ever alert for the makings of a bugaboo to scare the plain people. What lies under all this subservience is simple enough. The American, for all his braggadocio, is quite conscious of his intrinsic inferiority to the Englishman, on all cultural counts. He may put himself first as a man of business, as an adventurer in practical affairs or as a pioneer in the applied arts and sciences, but in all things removed from the mere pursuit of money and physical ease he well understands that he belongs at the second table. Even his recurrent attacks of Anglophobia are no more than Freudian evidences of his inferiority complex. He howls in order to still his inner sense of inequality, as he howls against imaginary enemies in order to convince himself that he is brave and against fabulous despotisms in order to prove that he is free. The Englishman is never deceived by this hocus-pocus. He knows that it is always possible to fetch the rebel back into camp by playing upon his elemental fears and vanities. A few dark threats, a few patronizing speeches, a few Oxford degrees, and the thing is done. More, the English scarcely regard it as hunting in the grand manner; it is a business of subalterns. When, during the early stages of the war, they had occasion to woo the American intelligentsia" what agents did they choose? Did they nominate Thomas Hardy, Joseph Conrad, George Moore and company? Nay, they nominated Conan Doyle, Coningsby Dawson, Alfred Noyes, Ian Hay, Chesterton, Kipling, Zangwill and company. In the choice there was high sagacity and no little oblique humor — as there was a bit later in the appointment of Lord Reading and Sir Auckland Geddes to Washington. The valuation they set upon the *aluminados* of the Republic was exactly the valuation they were in the habit of setting, at home, upon MM. of the Free Church Federation. They saw the eternal green-grocer beneath the master's gown and mortarboard. Let us look closely and we shall see him, too.

The essence of a self-reliant and autonomous culture is an unshakable egoism. It must not only regard itself as the peer of any other culture; it must regard itself as the superior of any other. You will find this indomitable pride in the culture of any truly first-rate nation: France, Germany or England. But you will not find it in the so-called culture of

America' Here the decadent Anglo-Saxon majority still looks obediently and a bit wistfully toward the motherland. No good American ever seriously questions an English judgment on an esthetic question, or even on an ethical, philosophical or political question. There is, in fact, seldom any rational reason why he should: it is almost always more mature, more tolerant, more intelligent than any judgment hatched 'at home. Behind it lies a settled scheme of things, a stable point of view, the authority of a free intellectual aristocracy, the pride of tradition and of power. The English are sure-footed, well-informed, persuasive. It is beyond their imagination that any one should seriously challenge them. In this overgrown and oafish colony there is no such sureness. The American always secretly envies the Englishman, even when he professes to flout him. The Englishman never envies the American.

The extraordinary colonist, moved to give utterance to the ideas bubbling within him, is thus vastly handicapped, for he must submit them to the test of a culture that, in the last analysis, is never quite his own culture, despite its dominance. Looking within himself, he finds that he is different, that he diverges from the English standard, that he is authentically American — and to be authentically American is to be officially inferior. He thus faces dismay at the very start: support is lacking when he needs it most In the motherland — in any motherland, in any wholly autonomous nation — there is a class of men like himself, devoted to translating the higher manifestations of the national spirit into ideas — men differing enormously among themselves, but still united in common cause against the lethargy and credulity of the mass. But in a colony that class, if it exists at all, lacks coherence and certainty; its authority is not only disputed by the inertia and suspiciousness of the lower orders, but also by the superior authority overseas; it is timorous and fearful of challenge. Thus it affords no protection to an individual of assertive originality, and he is forced to go as a suppliant to a quarter in which nothing is his by right, but everything must go by favor — in brief to a quarter where his very application must needs be regarded as an admission of his inferiority. The burden of proof upon him is thus made double. Obviously, he must be a man of very strong personality to surmount such obstacles triumphantly. Such strong men, of course, sometimes appear in a colony, but they always stand alone; their worst opposition is at home. For a colonial of less vigorous soul the battle is almost hopeless. Either he submits to subordination and so wears docilely the inferior badge of a praiseworthy and tolerated colonist, or he deserts the minority for the far more hospitable and confident majority, and so becomes a mere mob-artist.

Examples readily suggest themselves. I give you Poe and Whitman as men strong enough to weather the adverse wind. The salient thing about each of these men was this: that his impulse to self-expression, the force of his "obscure, inner necessity," was so powerful that it carried him beyond all ordinary ambitions and prudences — in other words, that the ego functioned so heroically that it quite disregarded the temporal welfare of the individual. Neither Poe nor Whitman made the slightest concession to what was the predominant English taste, the prevailing English authority, of his time. And neither yielded in the slightest to the maudlin echoes of English notions that passed for ideas in the United States; in neither will you find any recognizable reflection of the things that Americans were saying and doing all about them. Even Whitman, preaching democracy, preached a democracy that not one actual democrat in a hundred thousand could so much as imagine. What happened? Imprimis, English authority, at the start, dismissed them loftily; they were, at best, simply rare freaks from the colonies. Secondly, American stupidity, falling into step, came near overlooking them altogether. The accident that maintained them was an accident of personality and environment.

They happened to be men accustomed to social isolation and of the most meager wants, and it was thus difficult to deter them by neglect and punishment. So they stuck to their guns — and presently they were "'discovered" as the phrase is, by men of a culture wholly foreign to them and perhaps incomprehensible to them, and thereafter, by slow stages, they began to win a slow and reluctant recognition in England (at first only from rebels and iconoclasts), and finally even in America. That either, without French prompting, would have come to his present estate I doubt very much. And in support of that doubt I cite again the fact that Poe's high talents as a critic, not having interested the French, have never got their deserts either in England or at home.

It is lesser men that we chiefly have to deal with in this world, and it is among lesser men that the lack of a confident intellectual viewpoint in America makes itself most evident. Examples are numerous and obvious. On the one hand, we have Fenimore Cooper first making a cringing bow for English favor, and then, on being kicked out, joining the mob against sense; he wrote books so bad that even the Americans of 1830 admired them. On the other hand, we have Henry James, a deserter made by despair; one so depressed by the tacky company at the American first table that he preferred to sit at the second table of the English. The impulse was, and is common; it was only the forthright act that distinguished him. And in the middle ground, showing both seductions plainly, there is Mark Twain — at one moment striving his hardest for the English imprimatur, and childishly delighted by every favorable gesture; at the next, returning to the native mob as its premier clown — monkey-shining at banquets, cavorting in the newspapers, shrinking poltroonishly from his own ideas, obscenely eager to give no offense. A much greater artist than either Poe or Whitman, so I devoutly believe, but a good deal lower as a man. The ultimate passion was not there; the decent householder always pulled the ear of the dreamer. His fate has irony in it. In England they patronize him: he is, for an American, not so bad. In America, appalled by his occasional ascents to honesty, his stray impulses to be wholly himself, the dunderheads return him to arm's length, his old place, and one of the most eminent of them, writing in the New York Times, argues piously that it is impossible to imagine him actually believing the commonplace heresies he put into "What Is Man?"

11. Epilogue

I have described the disease. Let me say at once that I have no remedy lo offer. I simply set down a few ideas, throw out a few hints, attempt a few modest inquiries into causes. Perhaps my argument often turns upon itself: the field is weed-grown and paths are hard to follow. It may be that insurmountable natural obstacles stand in the way of the development of a distinctively American culture, grounded upon a truly egoistic nationalism and supported by a native aristocracy. After all, there is no categorical imperative that ordains it. In such matters, when the conditions are right, nature often arranges a division of labor. A nation shut in by racial and linguistic isolation — a Sweden, a Holland or a France — is forced into autonomy by sheer necessity; if it is to have any intellectual life at all it must develop its own. But that is not our case. There is England to hold up the torch for us, as France holds it up for Belgium, and Spain for Latin America, and Germany for Switzerland. It is our function, as the younger and less confident partner, to do the simpler, rougher parts of the joint labor — to develop the virtues of the more elemental orders of men: industry, piety, docility, endurance, assiduity and ingenuity in practical affairs — the wood-hewing and water-drawing of the race. It seems to me that we do all this very well; in these things we are better than the English. But when it comes to those larger and more difficult activities which concern only the superior minority, and are, in essence, no more than products of its efforts to demonstrate its superiority — when it comes to the higher varieties of speculation and self-expression, to the fine arts and the game of ideas — then we fall into a bad second place. Where we stand, intellectually, is where the English non-conformists stand; like them, we are marked by a fear of ideas as disturbing and corrupting. Our art is imitative and timorous. Our political theory is hopelessly sophomoric and superficial; even English Toryism and Russian Bolshevism are infinitely more profound and penetrating. And of the two philosophical systems that we have produced, one is so banal that it is now imbedded in the New Thought, and the other is so shallow that there is nothing in it either to puzzle or to outrage a school-marm.

Nevertheless, hope will not down, and now and then it is supported by something rather more real than mere desire. One observes an under-current of revolt, small but vigorous, and sometimes it exerts its force, not only against the superficial banality but also against the fundamental flabbiness, the intrinsic childishness of the Puritan *Anschauung*. The remedy for that childishness is skepticism, and already skepticism shows itself: in the iconoclastic political realism of Harold Steams, Waldo Frank and company, in the groping questions of Dreiser, Cabell and Anderson, in the operatic rebellions of the Village. True imagination, I often think, is no more than a function of this skepticism. It is the dull man who is always sure, and the sure man who is always dull. The more a man dreams, the less he believes. A great literature is thus chiefly the product of doubting and inquiring minds in revolt against the immovable certainties of the nation. Shakespeare, at a time of rising democratic feeling in England, flung the whole force of his genius against democracy. Cervantes, at a time when all Spain was romantic, made a headlong attack upon romance. Goethe, with Germany groping toward nationalism, threw his influences on the side of internationalism. The central trouble with America is conformity, timorousness, lack of enterprise and audacity. A nation of third-rate men, a land offering hospitality only to fourth-rate artists. In Elizabethan England they would have bawled for democracy, in the Spain of Cervantes they would have yelled for chivalry, and in the Germany of Goethe they would have wept and beat their breasts for the Fatherland. To-day, as in the day of Emerson, they set the tune. . . . But into the singing there occasionally enters a discordant note. On some dim to-morrow, perhaps, perchance, peradventure, they may be challenged.

II. ROOSEVELT: AN AUTOPSY

ONE thinks of Dr. Woodrow Wilson's biography of George Washington as of one of the strangest of all the world's books. Washington: the first, and perhaps also the last American gentleman. Wilson: the self -bamboozled Presbyterian, the right-thinker, the great moral statesman, the perfect model of the Christian cad. It is as if the Rev. Dr. Billy Sunday should do a biography of Charles Darwin — almost as if Dr. Wilson himself should dedicate his senility to a life of the Chevalier Bayard, or the Cid, or Christ. . . • But such phenomena, of course, are not actually rare in the republic; here everything happens that is forbidden by the probabilities and the decencies. The chief native critic of beautiful letters, for a whole generation, was a Baptist clergyman; he was succeeded by a literary Wall Street man, who gave way, in turn, to a soviet of ninth-rate pedagogues; this very curious apostolic succession I have already discussed. The dean of the music critics, even to-day, is a translator of grand opera libretti, and probably one of the worst that ever lived. Return, now, to political biography. Who can think of anything in American literature comparable to Morley's life of Gladstone, or Trevelyan's life of Macaulay, or Carlyle's Frederick, or even Winston Churchill's life of his father? I dredge my memory hopelessly; only William Graham Sumner's study of Andrew Jackson emerges — an extraordinarily astute and careful piece of work by one of the two most underestimated Americans of his generation, the other being Daniel Coit Oilman. But where is the first-rate biography of Washington — sound, fair, penetrating, honest, done by a man capable of comprehending the English gentry of the eighteenth century? And how long must we wait for adequate treatises upon Jefferson, Hamilton, Sam Adams, Aaron Burr, Henry Clay, Calhoun, Webster, Sumner, Grant, Sherman, Lee?

Even Lincoln is yet to be got vividly between the covers of a book. The Nicolay-Hay work is quite impossible; it is not a biography, but simply a huge storehouse of biographical raw materials; whoever can read it can also read the official Records of the Rebellion. All the other standard lives of old Abe — for instance, those of Lamon, Herndon and Weil, Stoddard, Morse and Miss Tarbell — fail still worse; when they are not grossly preachy and disingenuous they are trivial. So far as I can make out, no genuinely scientific study of the man has ever been attempted. The amazing conflict of testimony about him remains a conflict; the most elemental facts are yet to be established; he grows vaguer and more fabulous as year follows year. One would think that, by this time, the question of his religious views (to take one example) ought to be settled, but apparently it is not, for no longer than a year ago there came a reverend author. Dr. William E. Barton, with a whole volume upon the subject, and I was as much in the dark after reading it as I had been before I opened it. All previous biographers, it appeared by this author's evidence, had either dodged the problem, or lied. The official doctrine, in this as in other departments, is obviously quite unsound. One hears in the Sunday-schools that Abe was an austere and pious fellow, constantly taking the name of God in whispers, just as one reads in the school history-books that he was a shining idealist, holding all his vast powers by the magic of an inner and ineffable virtue. Imagine a man getting on in American politics, interesting and enchanting the boobery, sawing off the horns of other politicians, elbowing his way through primaries and conventions, by the magic of virtue! As well talk of fetching the mob by hawking exact and arctic justice! Abe, in fact, must have been a fellow highly skilled at the great democratic art of gum-shoeing. I like to think of him as one who defeated such politicians as Stanton, Douglas and Sumner with their own weapons — deftly leading them into ambuscades, boldly pulling their noses, magnificently ham-stringing and horn swoggling them— in brief, as a politician of extraordinary talents, who loved the game for its own sake, and had the measure of the crowd. His official portraits, both in prose and in daguerreotype, show him wearing the mien of a man about to be hanged; one never sees him smiling. Nevertheless, one hears that, until he emerged from Illinois, they always put the women, children and clergy to bed when he got a few gourds of com aboard, and it is a matter of unescapable record that his career in the State Legislature was indistinguishable from that of a Tammany Nietzsche. But, as I say, it is hopeless to look for the real man in the biographies of him: they are all full of distortion, chiefly pious and sentimental. The defect runs through the whole of American political biography, and even through the whole of American history. Nearly all our professional historians are poor men holding college posts, and they are ten times more cruelly beset by the ruling politico-plutocratic-social oligarchy than ever the Prussian professors were by the Hohenzollems. Let them diverge in the slightest from what is the current official doctrine, and they are turned out of their chairs with a ceremony suitable for the expulsion of a drunken valet. During the recent war a herd of two thousand and five hundred such miserable slaves was organized by Dr. Creel to lie for their country, and they at once fell upon the congenial task of rewriting American history to make it accord with the ideas of H. P. Davison, Admiral Sims, Nicholas Murray Butler, the Astors, Barney Baruch and Lord Northcliffe. It was a committee of this herd that solemnly pledged the honor of American scholarship to the authenticity of the celebrated Sisson documents. . • .

In the face of such acute military imbecility it is not surprising to discover that all of the existing biographies of the late Colonel Roosevelt — and they have been rolling off the presses at a dizzy rate since his death — are feeble, inaccurate, ignorant and preposterous. I have read, I suppose, at least ten of these tomes during the past year or so, and in all of them I have found vastly more gush than sense. Lawrence Abbott's "Impressions of Theodore Roosevelt' and William Roscoe Thayer's "Theodore Roosevelt may well serve as specimens. Abbott's book is the composition, not of an unbiased student of the man, but of a sort of groom of the hero. He is so extremely eager to prove that Roosevelt was the perfect right-thinker, according to the transient definitions of right-thinking, that he manages to get a flavor of dubiousness into his whole chronicle. I find myself doubting him even when I know that he is honest and suspect that he is right. As for Thayer, all he offers is a hasty and hollow pot-boiler — such a work as might have been well within the talents of, say, the late Murat Halstead or the editor of the New York Times. This Thayer has been heavily praised of late as the Leading American Biographer, and one constantly hears that some new university has made him Legum Doctor " or that he has been awarded a medal by this or that learned society, or that the post has brought him a new ribbon from some literary potentate in foreign parts. If, in fact, he is actually the cock of the walk in biography, then all I have said against American biographers is too mild and mellow. What one finds in his book is simply the third-rate correctness of a Boston colonial. Consider, for example, his frequent discussions of the war — a necessity in any work on Roosevelt. In England there is the mob's view of the war, and there is the view of civilized and intelligent men, e. g., Lansdowne, Lorebum, Austin Harrison, Morel, Keynes, Haldane, Hirst, Balfour, Robert Cecil. In New England, it would appear, the two views coalesce, with the first outside. There is scarcely a line on the subject in Thayer's book that might not have been written by Horatio Bottomley. . .

Obviously, Roosevelt's reaction to the war must occupy a large part of any adequate biography of him, for that reaction was probably more comprehensively typical of the man than any other business of his life. It displayed not only his whole stock of political principles, but also his whole stock of political tricks. It plumbed, on the one hand, the depths of his sagacity, and on the other hand the depths of his insincerity. Fundamentally, I am convinced, he was quite out of sympathy with, and even quite unable to comprehend the body of doctrine upon which the Allies, and later the United States, based their case. To him it must have seemed insane when it was not hypocritical, and hypocritical when it was not insane. His instincts were profoundly against a new loosing of democratic fustian upon the world; he believed in strongly centralized states, founded upon power and devoted to enterprises far transcending mere internal government; he was an imperialist of the type of Cecil Rhodes, Treitschke and Delcasse. But the fortunes of domestic politics jockeyed him into the position of standing as the spokesman of an almost exactly contrary philosophy. The visible enemy before him was Wilson. What he wanted as a politician was something that he could get only by wresting it from Wilson, and Wilson was too cunning to yield it without making a tremendous fight, chiefly by chicane — whooping for peace while preparing for war, playing mob fear against mob fear, concealing all his genuine motives and desires beneath clouds of chautauqual rhetoric, leading a mad dance whose tune changed at every swing. Here was an opponent that more than once puzzled Roosevelt, and in the end flatly dismayed him. Here was a mob-master with a technique infinitely more subtle and effective than his own. So lured into an unequal combat, the Rough Rider got bogged in absurdities so immense that only the democratic anaesthesia to absurdity saved him. To make any progress at all he was forced into fighting against his own side. He passed from the scene bawling piteously for a cause that, at bottom, it is impossible to imagine him believing in, and in terms of a philosophy that was as foreign to his true faith as it was to the faith of Wilson. In the whole affair there was a colossal irony. Both contestants were intrinsically frauds.

The fraudulence of Wilson is now admitted by all save a few survivors of the old corps of official pressagents, most of them devoid of both honesty and intelligence. No unbiased man, in the presence of the revelations of Bullitt, Keynes and a hundred other witnesses, and of the Russian and Shantung performances, and of innumerable salient domestic phenomena, can now believe that the *Doctor dulcifluus* was ever actually in favor of any of the brummagem ideals he once wept for, to the edification of a moral universe. They were, at best, no more than ingenious ruses de guerre" and even in the day of their widest credit it was the Espionage Act and the Solicitor-General to the Postoffice, rather than any plausibility in their substance, that got them their credit. In Roosevelt's case the imposture is less patent; he died before it was fully unmasked. What is more, his death put an end to whatever investigation of it was under way, for American sentimentality holds that it is indecent to inquire into the weaknesses of the dead, at least until all the flowers have withered on their tombs. When, a year ago, I ventured in a magazine article to call attention to Roosevelt's philosophical kinship to the Kaiser I received letters of denunciation from all parts of the United States, and not a few forthright demands that I recant on penalty of lynch law. Prudence demanded that I heed these demands. We live in a curious and often unsafe country. Haled before a Roosevelt judge for speeding my automobile, or spitting on the sidewalk, or carrying a jug, I might have been railroaded for ten years under some constructive corollary of the Espionage Act. But there were two things that supported me in my contumacy to the departed. One was a profound reverence for and fidelity to the truth, sometimes almost amounting to fanaticism. The other was the support of my venerable brother in epistemology, the eminent Iowa right-thinker and patriot. Prof. Dr. S. P. Sherman. Writing in the Nation" where he survives from more seemly days than these. Prof. Dr. Sherman put the thing in plain terms. "With the essentials in the religion of the militarists of Germany," he said, "Roosevelt was utterly in sympathy."

Utterly? Perhaps the adverb is a bit too strong. There was in the man a certain instinctive antipathy to the concrete aristocrat and in particular to the aristocrat's private code — the product, no doubt, of his essentially bourgeois origin and training. But if he could not go with the Junkers all the way, he could at least go the whole length of their distrust of the third order — the undifferentiated masses of men below. Here, I daresay, he owed a lot to Nietzsche. He was always reading German books, and among them, no doubt, were "Also sprach Zarathustra" and "Jenseits von Gut und Bose." In fact, the echoes were constantly sounding in his own harangues. Years ago, as an intellectual exercise while confined to hospital, I devised and printed a give-away of the Rooseveltian philosophy in parallel columns — in one column, extracts from "The Strenuous Life"; in the other, extracts from Nietzsche. The borrowings were numerous and unescapable. Theodore had swallowed Friedrich as a peasant swallows Peruna — bottle, cork, label and testimonials.

Worse, the draft whetted his appetite, and soon he was swallowing the Kaiser of the Garde-Kavallerie-mess and battleshiplaunching speeches — another somewhat defective Junker. In his palmy days it was often impossible to distinguish his politico-theological bulls from those of Wilhelm; during the war, indeed, I suspect that some of them were boldly lifted by the British press bureau, and palmed off as felonious imprudences out of Potsdam. Wilhelm was his model in Wellpolitiky and in sociology, exegetics, administration, law, sport and connubial polity no less. Both roared for doughty armies, eternally prepared — for the theory that the way to prevent war is to make all conceivable enemies think twice, thrice, ten times. Both dreamed of gigantic navies, with battleships as long as Brooklyn Bridge. Both preached incessantly the duty of the citizen to the state, with the soft pedal upon the duty of the state to the citizen. Both praised the habitually gravid wife. Both delighted in the armed pursuit of the lower fauna. Both heavily patronized the fine arts. Both were intimates of God, and announced His desires with authority. Both believed that all men who stood opposed to them were prompted by the devil and would suffer for it in hell. If, in fact, there was any difference between them, it was all in favor of Wilhelm. For one thing, he made very much fewer speeches; it took some colossal event, such as the launching of a dreadnaught or the birthday of a colonel-general, to get him upon his legs; the Reichstag was not constantly deluged with his advice and upbraiding. For another thing, he was a milder and more modest man—one more accustomed, let us say, to circumstance and authority, and hence less intoxicated by the greatness of his state. Finally, he had been trained to think, not only of his own immediate fortunes, but also of the remote interests of a family that, in his most expansive days, promised to hold the throne for many years, and so he cultivated a certain prudence, and even a certain ingratiating suavity. He could, on occasion, be extremely polite to an opponent. But Roosevelt was never polite to an opponent; perhaps a gentleman, by American standards, he was surely never a gentle man. In a political career of nearly forty years he was never even fair to an opponent. All of his gabble about the square deal was merely so much protective coloration, easily explicable on elementary Freudian grounds.

No man, facing Roosevelt in the heat of controversy, ever actually got a square deal. He took extravagant advantages; he played to the worst idiocies of the mob; he hit below the belt almost habitually. One never thinks of him as a duelist, say of the school of Disraeli, Palmerston and, to drop a bit, Blaine. One always thinks of him as a glorified longshoreman engaged eternally in cleaning out bar-rooms — and not too proud to gauge when the inspiration came to him, or to bite in the clinches, or to oppose the relatively fragile brass knuckles of the code with chair-legs, bung-starters, cuspidors, demijohns, and icepicks.

Abbott and Thayer, in their books, make elaborate efforts to depict their hero as one born with a deep loathing of the whole Prussian scheme of things, and particularly of the Prussian technique in combat. Abbott even goes so far as to hint that the attentions of the Kaiser, during Roosevelt's historic tour of Europe on his return from Africa, were subtly revolting to him. Nothing could be more absurd. Prof. Dr. Sherman, in the article I have mentioned, blows up that nonsense by quoting from a speech made by the tourist in Berlin — a speech arguing for the most extreme sort of militarism in a manner that must have made even some of the Junkers blow their noses dubiously. The disproof need not be piled up; the America that Roosevelt dreamed of was always a sort of swollen Prussia, truculent without and regimented within. There was always a clank of the saber in his discourse; he could not discuss the tamest matter without swaggering in the best dragoon fashion. Abbott gets into yet deeper waters when he sets up the doctrine that the invasion of Belgium threw his darling into an instantaneous and tremendous fit of moral indignation, and that the curious delay in the public exhibition thereof, so much discussed since, was due to his (Abbott's) fatuous interference — a *faux pas* later regretted with much bitterness. Unluckily, the evidence he offers leaves me full of doubts. What the doctrine demands that one believe is simply this: that the man who, for mere commercial advantage and (in Frederick's famous phrase) "to make himself talked of in the world," tore up the treaty of 1848 between the United States and Colombia (geb. New Granada), whereby the United States forever guaranteed the "sovereignty and ownership" of the Colombians in the isthmus of Panama — that this same man, thirteen years later, was horrified into a fever when Germany, facing powerful foes on two fronts, tore up the treaty of 1832, guaranteeing, not the sovereignty, but the bald neutrality of Belgium — a neutrality already destroyed, according to the evidence before the Germans, by Belgium's own acts.

It is hard, without an inordinate strain upon the credulity, to believe any such thing, particularly in view of the fact that this instantaneous indignation of the most impulsive and vocal of men was diligently concealed for at least six weeks, with reporters camped upon his doorstep day and night, begging him to say the very thing that he left so darkly unsaid. Can one imagine Roosevelt, with red-fire raging within him and sky-rockets bursting in his veins, holding his peace for a month and a half? I have no doubt whatever that Abbott, as he says, desired to avoid embarrassing Dr. Wilson — but think of Roosevelt showing any such delicacy! For one, I am not equal to the feat. All that unprecedented reticence, in fact, is far more readily explicable on other and less lofty grounds. What really happened I presume to guess. My guess is that Roosevelt, like the great majority of other Americans, was not instantly and automatically outraged by the invasion of Belgium. On the contrary, he probably viewed it as a regrettable, but not unexpected or unparalleled device of war—if anything, as something rather thrillingly gaudy and effective—a fine piece of virtuosity, pleasing to a military connoisseur. But then came the deluge of Belgian atrocity stories, and the organized campaign to enlist American sympathies. It succeeded very quickly. By the middle of August the British press bureau was in full swing; by the beginning of September the country was flooded with inflammatory stuff; six weeks after the war opened it was already hazardous for a German in America to state his country's case. Meanwhile, the Wilson administration had declared for neutrality, and was still making a more or less sincere effort to practice it, at least on the surface. Here was Roosevelt's opportunity, and he leaped to it with sure instinct. On the one side was the administration that he detested, and that all his self-interest (e. g., his yearning to get back his old leadership and to become President again in 1917) prompted him to deal a mortal blow, and on the other side was a ready-made issue, full of emotional possibilities, stupendously pumped up by extremely clever propaganda, and so far unembraced by any other rabble-rouser of the first magnitude. Is it any wonder that he gave a whoop, jumped upon his cayuse, and began screaming for war? In war lay the greatest chance of his life. In war lay the con- fusion and destruction of Wilson, and the melodramatic renaissance of the Rough Rider, the professional hero, the national Barbarossa.

In all this, of course, I strip the process of its plumes and spangles, and expose a chain of causes and effects that Roosevelt himself, if he were alive, would denounce as grossly contumelious to his native purity of spirit — and perhaps in all honesty. It is not necessary to raise any doubts as to that honesty. No one who has given any study to the developement and propagation of political doctrine in the United States can have failed to notice how the belief in issues among politicians tends to run in exact ratio to the popularity of those issues. Let the populace begin suddenly to swallow a new panacea or to take fright at a new bugaboo, and almost instantly ninetenths of the master-minds of politics begin to believe that the panacea is a sure cure for all the malaises of the republic, and the bugaboo an immediate and unbearable menace to all law, order and domestic tranquillity. At the bottom of this singular intellectual resilience, of course, there is a good deal of hard calculation; a man must keep up with the procession of crazes, or his day is swiftly done. But in it there are also considerations a good deal more subtle, and maybe less discreditable. For one thing, a man devoted professionally to patriotism and the wisdom of the fathers is very apt to come to a resigned sort of acquiescence in all the doctrinaire rubbish that lies beneath the national scheme of things — to believe, let us say, if not that the plain people are gifted with an infallible sagacity, then at least that they have an inalienable right to see their follies executed. Poll-parroting nonsense as a matter of daily routine, the politician ends by assuming that it is sense, even though he doesn't believe it. For another thing, there is the contagion of mob enthusiasm — a much underestimated murrain. We all saw what it could do during the war — college professors taking their tune from the yellow journals, the rev. clergy performing in the pulpit like so many Liberty Loan orators in five-cent moving-picture houses, hysteria grown epidemic like the influenza. No man is so remote and arctic that he is wholly safe from that contamination; it explains many extravagant phenomena of a democratic society; in particular, it explains why the mob leader is so often a victim to his mob.

Roosevelt, a perfectly typical politician, devoted to the trade, not primarily because he was gnawed by ideals, but because he frankly enjoyed its rough-and-tumble encounters and its gaudy rewards, was probably moved in both ways — and also by the hard calculation that I have mentioned. If, by any ineptness of the British press-agents, tear-squeezers and orphan-exhibitors, indignation over the invasion of Belgium had failed to materialize — if, worse still, some gross infringement of American rights by the English had caused it to be forgotten completely — if, finally, Dr. Wilson had been whooping for war with the populace firmly against him — in such event it goes without saying that the moral horror of Dr. Roosevelt would have stopped short at a very low amperage, and that he would have refrained from making it the center of his polity. But with things as they were, lying neatly to his hand, he permitted it to take on an extraordinary virulence, and before long all his old delight in German militarism had been converted into a lofty detestation of German militarism, and its chief spokesman on this side of the Atlantic became its chief opponent. Getting rid of that old delight, of course, was not easily achieved. The concrete enthusiasm could be throttled, but the habit of mind remained. Thus one beheld the curious spectacle of militarism belabored in terms of militarism — of the Kaiser arraigned in unmistakably kaiserliche tones.

Such violent swallowings and regurgitations were no novelties to the man. His whole political career was marked, in fact, by performances of the same sort The issues that won him most votes were issues that, at bottom, he didn't believe in; there was always a mental reservation in his rhetoric. He got into politics, not as a tribune of the plain people, but as an amateur reformer of the snobbish type common in the eighties, by the Nation out of the Social Register. He was a young Harvard man scandalized by the discovery that his town was run by men with such names as Michael O'Shaunnessy and Terence Googan — that his social inferiors were his political superiors. His sympathies were essentially anti-democratic. He had a high view of his private position as a young fellow of wealth and education. He believed in strong centralization — the concentration of power in a few hands, the strict regimentation of the nether herd, the abandonment of democratic platitudes. His heroes were such Federalists as Morris and Hamilton; he made his first splash in the world by writing about them and praising them. Worse, his daily associations were with the old Union League crowd of high-tariff Republicans — men almost apoplectically opposed to every movement from below — safe and sane men, highly conservative and suspicious men — the profiteers of peace, as they afterward became the profiteers of war. His early adventures in politics were not very fortunate, nor did they reveal any capacity for leadership. The bosses of the day took him in rather humorously, played him for what they could get out of him, and then turned him loose. In a few years he became disgusted and went West. Returning after a bit, he encountered catastrophe: as a candidate for Mayor of New York he was drubbed unmercifully. He went back to the West. He was, up to this time, a comic figure — an anti-politician victimized by politicians, a pseudo-aristocrat made ridiculous by the mob-masters he detested. But meanwhile something was happening that changed the whole color of the political scene, and was destined, eventually, to give Roosevelt his chance. That something was a shifting in what might be called the foundations of reform. Up to now it had been an essentially aristocratic movement—superior, sniffish and anti-democratic. But hereafter it took on a strongly democratic color and began to adopt democratic methods. More, the change gave it new life. What Harvard, the Union League Club and the Nation had failed to accomplish, the plain people now undertook to accomplish. This invasion of the old citadel of virtue was first observed in the West, and its manifestations out there must have given Roosevelt a good deal more disquiet than satisfaction. It is impossible to imagine him finding anything to his taste in the outlandish doings of the Populists, the wild schemes of the pre-Bryan dervishes. His instincts were against all that sort of thing. But as the movement spread toward the East it took on a certain urbanity, and by the time it reached the seaboard it had begun to be quite civilized. With this new brand of reform Roosevelt now made terms. It was full of principles that outraged all his pruderies, but it at least promised to work. His entire political history thereafter, down to the day of his death, was a history of compromises with the new forces — of a gradual yielding, for strategic purposes, to ideas that were intrinsically at odds with his congenital prejudices. When, after a generation of that sort of compromising, the so-called Progressive party was organized and he seized the leadership of it from the Westerners who had founded it, he performed a feat of wholesale englutination that must forever hold a high place upon the roll of political prodigies. That is to say, he swallowed at one gigantic gulp, and out of the same herculean jug, the most amazing mixture of social, political and economic perunas ever got down by one hero, however valiant, however athirst — a cocktail made up of all the elixirs hawked among the boobery in his time, from woman suffrage to the direct primary, and from the initiative and referendum to the short ballot, and from prohibition to public ownership, and from trust-busting to the recall of judges.

This homeric achievement made him the head of the most tatterdemalion party ever seen in American politics — a party composed of such incompatible ingredients and hung together so loosely that it began to disintegrate the moment it was born. In part it was made up of mere disordered enthusiasts — believers in anything and everything, pathetic victims of the credulity complex, habitual followers of jitney messiahs, incurable hopers and snufflers. But in part it was also made up of rice converts like Roosevelt himself — men eager for office, disappointed by the old parties, and now quite willing to accept any aid that half -idiot doctrinaires could give them. I have no doubt that Roosevelt himself, carried away by the emotional storms of the moment and especially by the quasi-religious monkey-shines that marked the first Progressive convention, gradually convinced himself that at least some of the doctrinaires, in the midst of all their imbecility, yet preached a few ideas that were workable, and perhaps even sound. But at bottom he was against them, and not only in the matter of their specific sure cures, but also in the larger matter of their childish faith in the wisdom and virtue of the plain people. Roosevelt, for all his fluent mastery of democratic counter-words, democratic gestures and all the rest of the armamentarium of the mob-master, had no such faith m his heart of hearts. He didn't believe in democracy; he believed simply in government. His remedy for all the great pangs and longings of existence was not a dispersion of authority, but a hard concentration of authority. He was not in favor of unlimited experiment; he was in favor of a rigid control from above, a despotism of inspired prophets and policemen. He was not for democracy as his followers understood democracy, and as it actually is and must be; he was for a paternalism of the true Bismarckian pattern, almost of the Napoleonicor Ludendorffian pattern — a paternalism concerning itself with all things, from the regulation of coal-mining and meat-packing to the regulation of spelling and marital rights. His instincts were always those of the property-owning Tory, not those of the romantic Liberal. All the fundamental objects of Liberalism — free speech, unhampered enterprise, the least possible governmental interference — were abhorrent to him. Even when, for campaign purposes, he came to terms with the Liberals his thoughts always ranged far afield. When he tackled the trusts the thing that he had in his mind's eye was not the restoration of competition but the subordination of all private trusts to one great national trust, with himself at its head. And when he attacked the courts it was not because they put their own prejudice before the law but because they refused to put his prejudices before the law.

In all his career no one ever heard him make an argument for the rights of the citizen; his eloquence was always expended in expounding the duties of the citizen. I have before me a speech in which he pleaded for "a spirit of kindly justice toward every man and woman," but that seems to be as far as he ever got in that direction — and it was the gratuitous justice of the absolute monarch that he apparently had in mind, not the autonomous and inalienable justice of a free society. The duties of the citizen, as he understood them, related not only to acts, but also to thoughts. There was, to his mind, a simple body of primary doctrine, and dissent from it was the foulest of crimes. No man could have been more bitter against opponents, or more unfair to them, or more ungenerous. In this department, indeed, even so gifted a specialist in dishonorable controversy as Dr. Wilson has seldom surpassed him. He never stood up to a frank and chivalrous debate. He dragged herrings across the trail. He made seductive faces at the gallery. He capitalized his enormous talents as an entertainer, his rank as a national hero, his public influence and consequence. The two great law-suits in which he was engaged were screaming burlesques upon justice. He tried them in the newspapers before ever they were called; he befogged them with irrelevant issues; his appearances in court were not the appearances of a witness standing on a level with other witnesses, but those of a comedian sure of his crowd. He was, in his dealings with concrete men as in his dealings with men in the mass, a charlatan of the very highest skill — and there was in him, it goes without saying, the persuasive charm of the charlatan as well as the daring deviousness, the humanness of naivete as well as the humanness of chicane. He knew how to woo — and not only boobs. He was, for all his ruses and ambuscades, a jolly fellow.

It seems to be forgotten that the current American theory that political heresy should be put down by force, that a man who disputes whatever is official has no rights in law or equity, that he is lucky if he fares no worse than to lose his constitutional benefits of free speech, free assemblage and the use of the mails — it seems to be forgotten that this theory was invented, not by Dr. Wilson, but by Roosevelt. Most Liberals, I suppose" would credit it, if asked, to Wilson. He has carried it to extravagant lengths; he is the father superior of all the present advocates of it; he will probably go down into American history as its greatest prophet. But it was first clearly stated, not in any Wilsonian bull to the right-thinkers of all lands, but in Roosevelt's proceedings against the so-called Paterson anarchists. You will find it set forth at length in an opinion prepared for him by his Attorney-General, Charles J. Bonaparte, another curious and almost fabulous character, also an absolutist wearing the false whiskers of a democrat. Bonaparte furnished the law, and Roosevelt furnished the blood and iron. It was an almost ideal combination; Bonaparte had precisely the touch of Italian finesse that the Rough Rider always lacked. Roosevelt believed in the Paterson doctrine — in brief, that the Constitution does not throw its cloak around heretics — to the end of his days. In the face of what he conceived to be contumacy to revelation his fury lock on a sort of lyrical grandeur. There was nothing too awful for the culprit in the dock. Upon his head were poured denunciations as violent as the wildest interdicts of a mediaeval pope.

The appearance of such men, of course, is inevitable under a democracy. Consummate showmen, they arrest the wonder of the mob, and so put its suspicions to sleep. What they actually believe is of secondary consequence; the main thing is what they say; even more, the way they say it. Obviously, their activity does a great deal of damage to the democratic theory, for they are standing refutations of the primary doctrine that the common folk choose their leaders wisely. They damage it again in another and more subtle way. That is to say, their ineradicable contempt for the minds they must heat up and bamboozle leads them into a fatalism that shows itself in a cynical and opportunistic politics, a deliberate avoidance of fundamentals. The policy of a democracy thus becomes an eternal improvisation, changing with the private ambitions of its leaders and the transient and often unintelligible emotions of its rank and file. Roosevelt, incurably undemocratic in his habits of mind, often found it difficult to gauge those emotional oscillations. The fact explains his frequent loss of mob support, his periodical journeys into Coventry. There were times when his magnificent talents as a public comedian brought the proletariat to an almost unanimous groveling at his feet, but there were also times when he puzzled and dismayed it, and so awakened its hostility. When he assaulted Wilson on the neutrality issue, early in 1915, he made a quite typical mistake. That mistake consisted in assuming that public indignation over the wrongs of the Belgians would maintain itself at a high temperature — that it would develop rapidly into a demand for intervention. Roosevelt made himself the spokesman of that demand, and then found to his consternation that it was waning — that the great masses of the plain people, prospering under the Wilsonian neutrality, were inclined to preserve it, at no matter what cost to the Belgians. In 1915, after the Lusitania affair, things seemed to swing his way again, and he got vigorous support from the British press bureau. But in a few months he found himself once more attempting to lead a mob that was fast slipping away. Wilson, a very much shrewder politician, with little of Roosevelt's weakness for succumbing to his own rhetoric, discerned the truth much more quickly and clearly. In 1916 he made his campaign for reelection on a flatly anti-Roosevelt peace issue, and not only got himself reelected, but also drove Roosevelt out of the ring.

What happened thereafter deserves a great deal more careful study than it will ever get from the timorous eunuchs who posture as American historians. At the moment, it is the official doctrine in England, where the thing is more freely discussed than at home, that Wilson was forced into the war by an irresistible movement from below — that the plain people compelled him to abandon neutrality and move reluctantly upon the Germans. Nothing could be more untrue. The plain people, at the end of 1916, were in favor of peace, and they believed that Wilson was in favor of peace. How they were gradually worked up to complaisance and then to enthusiasm and then to hysteria and then to acute mania — this is a tale to be told in more leisurely days and by historians without boards of trustees on their necks. For the present purpose it is sufficient to note that the whole thing was achieved so quickly and so neatly that its success left Roosevelt surprised and helpless. His issue had been stolen from directly under his nose. He was left standing daunted and alone, a boy upon a burning deck. It took him months to collect his scattered wits, and even then his attack upon the administration was feeble and ineffective. To the plain people it seemed a mere ill-natured snapping at a successful rival, which in fact it was, and so they paid no heed to it, and Roosevelt found himself isolated once more. Thus he passed from the scene in the shadows, a broken politician and a disappointed man.

I have a notion that he died too soon. His best days were probably not behind him, but ahead of him. Had he lived ten years longer, he might have enjoyed a great rehabilitation, and exchanged his old false leadership of the inflammatory and fickle mob for a sound and true leadership of the civilized minority. For the more one studies his mountebankeries as mob-master, the more one is convinced that there was a shrewd man beneath the motley, and that his actual beliefs were anything but nonsensical. The truth of them, indeed, emerges more clearly day by day. The old theory of a federation of free and autonomous states has broken down by its own weight, and we are moved toward centralization by forces that have long been powerful and are now quite irresistible. So with the old theory of national isolation: it, too, has fallen to pieces. The United States can no longer hope to lead a separate life in the world, undisturbed by the pressure of foreign aspirations. We came out of the war to find ourselves hemmed in by hostilities that no longer troubled to conceal themselves, and if they are not as close and menacing today as those that have hemmed in Germany for centuries they are none the less plainly there and plainly growing. Roosevelt, by whatever route of reflection or intuition, arrived at a sense of these facts at a time when it was still somewhat scandalous to state them, and it was the capital effort of his life to reconcile them, in some dark way or other, to the prevailing platitudes, and so get them heeded. To-day no one seriously maintains, as all Americans once maintained, that the states can go on existing together as independent commonwealths, each with its own laws, its own legal theory and its own view of the common constitutional bond. And to-day no one seriously maintains, as all Americans once maintained, that the nation may safely potter on without adequate means of defense. However unpleasant it may be to contemplate, the fact is plain that the American people, during the next century, will have to fight to maintain their place in the sun.

Roosevelt lived just long enough to see his notions in these directions take on life, but not long enough to see them openly adopted. To the extent of his prevision he was a genuine leader of the nation, and perhaps in the years to come, when his actual ideas are disentangled from the demagogic fustian in which he had to wrap them, his more honest pronunciamentoes will be given canonical honors, and he will be ranked among the prophets. He saw clearly more than one other thing that was by no means obvious to his age — for example, the inevitability of frequent wars under the new world-system of extreme nationalism; again, the urgent necessity, for primary police ends, of organizing the backward nations into groups of vassals, each under the hoof of some first-rate power; yet again, the probability of the breakdown of the old system of free competition; once more, the high social utility of the Spartan virtues and the grave dangers of sloth and ease; finally, the incompatibility of free speech and democracy. I do not say that he was always quite honest, even when he was most indubitably right. But in so far as it was possible for him to be honest and exist at all politically, he inclined toward the straightforward thought and the candid word. That is to say, his instinct prompted him to tell the truth, just as the instinct of Dr. Wilson prompts him to shift and dissimulate. What ailed him was the fact that his lust for glory, when it came to a struggle, was always vastly more powerful than his lust for the eternal verities. Tempted sufficiently, he would sacrifice anything and everything to get applause. Thus the statesman was debauched by the politician, and the philosopher was elbowed out of sight by the popinjay.

Where he failed most miserably was in his remedies. A remarkably penetrating diagnostician, well-read, unprejudiced and with a touch of genuine scientific passion, he always stooped to quackery when he prescribed a course of treatment. For all his sensational attacks upon the trusts, he never managed to devise a scheme to curb them — and even when he sought to apply the schemes of other men he invariably corrupted the business with timorousness and insincerity. So with his campaign for national preparedness. He displayed the disease magnificently, but the course of medication that he proposed was vague and unconvincing; it was not, indeed, without justification that the plain people mistook his advocacy of an adequate army for a mere secret yearning to prance upon a chancer at the head of huge hordes. So, again, with his eloquent plea for national solidarity and an end of hyphenism. The dangers that he pointed out were very real and very menacing, but his plan for abating them only made them worse. His objurgations against the Germans surely accomplished nothing; the hyphenate of 1915 is still a hyphenate in his heart —

with bitter and unforgettable grievances to support him. Roosevelt, very characteristically, swung too far. In denouncing German hyphenism so extravagantly he contrived to give an enormous impetus to English hyphenism, a far older and more perilous malady. It has already gone so far that a large and influential party endeavors almost openly to convert the United States into a mere vassal state of England's. Instead of national solidarity following the war, we have only a revival of Know-Nothingism; one faction of hyphenates tries to exterminate another faction. Roosevelt's error here was one that he was always making. Carried away by the ease with which he could heat up the mob, he tried to accomplish instantly and by force majeure what could only be accomplished by a long and complex process, with more good will on both sides than ever so opinionated and melodramatic a pseudo- Junker was capable of. But though he thus made a mess of the cure, he was undoubtedly right about the disease.

The talented Sherman, in the monograph that I have praised, argues that the chief contribution of the dead gladiator to American life was the example of his gigantic gusto, his delight in toil and struggle, his superb aliveness. The fact is plain. What he stood most clearly in opposition to was the superior pessimism of the three Adams brothers — the notion that the public problems of a democracy are unworthy the thought and effort of a civilized and self-respecting man — the sad error that lies in wait for all of us who hold ourselves above the general. Against this suicidal aloofness Roosevelt always hurled himself with brave effect. Enormously sensitive and resilient, almost pathological in his appetite for activity, he made it plain to every one that the most stimulating sort of sport imaginable was to be obtained in fighting, not for mere money, but for ideas. There was no aristocratic reserve about him. He was not, in fact, an aristocrat at all, but a quite typical member of the upper bourgeoisie; his people were not patroons in New Amsterdam, but simple traders; he was himself a social pusher, and eternally tickled by the thought that he had had a Bonaparte in his cabinet. The marks of the thoroughbred were simply not there.

The man was blatant, crude, overly confidential, devious, tyrannical, vainglorious, sometimes quite childish. One often observed in him a certain pathetic wistfulness, a reaching out for a grand manner that was utterly beyond him. But the sweet went with the bitter. He had all the virtues of the fat and complacent burgher. His disdain of affectation and prudery was magnificent. He hated all pretension save his own pretension. He had a sound respect for hard effort, for loyalty, for thrift, for honest achievement.

His worst defects, it seems to me, were the defects of his race and time. Aspiring to be the leader of a nation of third-rate men, he had to stoop to the common level. When he struck out for realms above that level he always came to grief: this was the "unsafe" Roosevelt, the Roosevelt who was laughed at, the Roosevelt retired suddenly to cold storage. This was the Roosevelt who, in happier times and a better place» might have been. Well, one does what one can.

III THE SAHARA OF BOZART

Alas, for the South! Her books have grown fewer — She never was much given to literature.

IN the lamented J. Gordon Coogler, author of these elegaic lines, there was the insight of a true poet. He was the last bard of Dixie, at least in the legitimate line. Down there a poet is now almost as rare as an oboe-player, a dry-point etcher or a metaphysician. It is, indeed, amazing to contemplate so vast a vacuity. One thinks of the interstellar spaces, of the colossal reaches of the now mythical ether. Nearly the whole of Europe could be lost in that stupendous region of fat farms, shoddy cities and paralyzed cerebrums: one could throw in France, Germany and Italy, and still have room for the British Isles. And yet, for all its size and all its wealth and all the "progress" it babbles of, it is almost as sterile, artistically, intellectually, culturally, as the Sahara Desert. There are single acres in Europe that house more first-rate men than all the states south of the Potomac; there are probably single square miles in America. If the whole of the late Confederacy were to be engulfed by a tidal wave tomorrow, the effect upon the civilized minority of men in the world would be but little greater than that of a flood on the Yang-tse-kiang. It would be impossible in all history to match so complete a drying-up of a civilization.

I say a civilization because that is what, in the old days, the South had, despite the Baptist and Methodist barbarism that reigns down there now. More, it was a civilization of manifold excellences — perhaps the best that the Western Hemisphere has ever seen — undoubtedly the best that These States have ever seen. Down to the middle of the last century, and even beyond, the main hatchery of ideas on this side of the water was across the Potomac bridges. The New England shopkeepers and theologians never really developed a civilisation; all they ever developed was a government. They were, at their best, tawdry and tacky fellows, oafish in manner and devoid of imagination; one searches the books in vain for mention of a salient Yankee gentleman; as well look for a Welsh gentleman. But in the south there were men of delicate fancy, urbane instinct and aristocratic manner — in brief, superior men — in brief, gentry. To politics, their chief diversion, they brought active and original minds. It was there that nearly all the political theories we still cherish and suffer under came to birth. It was there that the crude dogmatism of New England was refined and humanized. It was there, above all, that some attention was given to the art of living — that life got beyond and above the state of a mere infliction and became an exhilarating experience. A certain noble spaciousness was in the ancient southern scheme of things. The Ur Confederate had leisure. He liked to toy with ideas. He was hospitable and tolerant He had the vague thing that we call culture.

But consider the condition of his late empire today. The picture gives one the creeps. It is as if the Civil War stamped out every last bearer of the torch, and left only a mob of peasants on the field. One thinks of Asia Minor, resigned to Armenians, Greeks and wild swine, of Poland abandoned to the Poles. In all that gargantuan paradise of the fourth-rate there is not a single picture gallery worth going into, or a single orchestra capable of playing the nine symphonies of Beethoven, or a single opera-house, or a single theater devoted to decent plays, or a single public monument (built since the war) that is worth looking at, or a single workshop devoted to the making of beautiful things. Once you have counted Robert Loveman (an Ohioan by birth) and John McClure (an Oklahoman) you will not find a single southern poet above the rank of a neighborhood rhymester. Once you have counted James Branch Cabell (a lingering survivor of the ancien regime: a scarlet dragonfly imbedded in opaque amber) you will not find a single southern prose writer who can actually write.

And once you have — but when you come to critics, musical composers, painters, sculptors, architects and the like, you will have to give it up, for there is not even a bad one between the Potomac mud-flats and the Gulf. Nor an historian. Nor a sociologist. Nor a philosopher. Nor a theologian. Nor a scientist. In all these fields the south is an awe-inspiring blank — a brother to Portugal, Serbia and Esthonia.

Consider, for example, the present estate and dignity of Virginia — in the great days indubitably the premier American state, the mother of Presidents and statesmen, the home of the first American university worthy of the name, the arbiter elegantiarum of the western world. Well, observe Virginia to-day. It is years since a first-rate man, save only Cabell, has come out of it; it is years since an idea has come out of it. The old aristocracy went down the red gullet of war; the poor white trash are now in the saddle. Politics in Virginia are cheap, ignorant, parochial, idiotic; there is scarcely a man in office above the rank of a professional job-seeker; the political doctrine that prevails is made up of hand-me-downs from the bumpkinry of the Middle West — Bryanism, Prohibition, vice crusading, all that sort of filthy claptrap; the administration of the law is turned over to professors of Puritanism and espionage; a Washington or a Jefferson, dumped there by some act of God, would be denounced as a scoundrel and jailed

overnight. Elegance, esprit, culture? Virginia has no art, no literature, no philosophy, no mind or aspiration of her own. Her education has sunk to the Baptist seminary level; not a single contribution to human knowledge has come out of her colleges in twenty-five years; she spends less than half upon her common schools, per capita, than any northern state spends. In brief, an intellectual Gobi or Lapland. Urbanity, politesse, chivalry? Go to! It was in Virginia that they invented the device of searching for contraband whisky in women's underwear. . . . There remains, at the top, a ghost of the old aristocracy, a bit wistful and infinitely charming. But it has lost all its old leadership to fabulous monsters from the lower depths; it is submerged in an industrial plutocracy that is ignorant and ignominious. The mind of the state, as it is revealed to the nation, is pathetically naive and inconsequential. It no longer reacts with energy and elasticity to great problems. It has fallen to the bombastic trivialities of the camp-meeting and the chautauqua. Its foremost exponent — if so flabby a thing may be said to have an exponent — is a stateman whose name is synonymous with empty words, broken pledges and false pretenses. One could no more imagine a Lee or a Washington in the Virginia of to-day than one could imagine a Huxley in Nicaragua.

I choose the Old Dominion, not because I disdain it, but precisely because I esteem it. It is, by long odds, the most civilized of the southern states, now as always. It has sent a host of creditable sons northward; the stream kept running into our own time. Virginians, even the worst of them, show the effects of a great tradition. They hold themselves above other southerners, and with sound pretension. If one turns to such a commonwealth as Georgia the picture becomes far darker. There the liberated lower orders of whites have borrowed the worst commercial bounderism of the Yankee and superimposed it upon a culture that, at bottom, is but little removed from savagery. Georgia is at once the home of the cotton-mill sweater and of the most noisy and vapid sort of chamber of commerce, of the Methodist parson turned Savonarola and of the lynching bee. A self-respecting European, going there to live, would not only find intellectual stimulation utterly lacking; he would actually feel a certain insecurity, as if the scene were the Balkans or the China Coast. The Leo Frank affair was no isolated phenomenon. It fitted into its frame very snugly. It was a natural expression of Georgian notions of truth and justice. There is a state with more than half the area of Italy and more population than either Denmark or Norway, and yet in thirty years it has not produced a single idea. Once upon a time a Georgian printed a couple of books that attracted notice, but immediately it turned out that he was little more than an amanuensis for the local blacks — that his works were really the products, not of white Georgia, but of black Georgia. Writing afterward as a white man, he swiftly subsided into the fifth rank. And he is not only the glory of the literature of Georgia; he is, almost literally, the whole of the literature of Georgia — nay, of the entire art of Georgia.

Virginia is the best of the south to-day, and Georgia is perhaps the worst. The one is simply senile; the other is crass, gross, vulgar and obnoxious. Between lies a vast plain of mediocrity, stupidity, lethargy, almost of dead silence. In the north, of course, there is also grossness, crassness, vulgarity. The north, in its way, is also stupid and obnoxious. But nowhere in the north is there such complete sterility, so depressing a lack of all civilized gesture and aspiration. One would find it difficult to unearth a second-rate city between the Ohio and the Pacific that isn't struggling to establish an orchestra, or setting up a little theater, or going in for an art gallery, or making some other effort to get into touch with civilization. These efforts often fail, and sometimes they succeed rather absurdly, but under them there is at least an impulse that deserves respect, and that is the impulse to seek beauty and to experiment with ideas, and so to give the life of every day a certain dignity and purpose. You will find no such impulse in the south.

There are no committees down there cadging subscriptions for orchestras; if a string quartet is ever heard there, the news of it has never come out; an opera troupe, when it roves the land, is a nine days' wonder. The little theater movement has swept the whole country, enormously augmenting the public interest in sound plays, giving new dramatists their chance, forcing reforms upon the commercial theater. Everywhere else the wave rolls high — but along the line of the Potomac it ' breaks upon a rock-bound shore. There is no little theater beyond. There is no gallery of pictures. No artist ever gives exhibitions. No one talks of such things. No one seems to be interested in such things.

As for the cause of this unanimous torpor and doltishness, this curious and almost pathological estrangement from everything that makes for a civilized culture, I have hinted at it already, and now state it again. The south has simply been drained of all its best blood. The vast blood-letting of the Civil War half exterminated and wholly paralyzed the old aristocracy, and so left the land to the harsh mercies of the poor white trash, now its masters. The war, of course, was not a complete massacre. It spared a decent number of first-rate southerners — perhaps even some of the very best. Moreover, other countries, notably France and Germany, have survived far more staggering butcheries, and even showed marked progress thereafter. But the war not only cost a great many valuable lives; it also brought bankruptcy, demoralization and despair in its train — and so the majority of the first-rate southerners that were left, broken in spirit and unable to live under the new dispensation, cleared out. A few went to South America, to Egypt, to the Far East. Most came north. They were fecund; their progeny is widely dispersed, to the great benefit of the north. A southerner of good blood almost always does well in the north. He finds, even in the big cities, surroundings fit for a man of condition. His peculiar qualities have a high social value, and are esteemed. He is welcomed by the codfish aristocracy as one palpably superior. But in the south he throws up his hands. It is impossible for him to stoop to the common level. He cannot brawl in politics with the grandsons of his grandfather's tenants. He is unable to share their fierce jealousy of the emerging black — the cornerstone of all their public thinking. He is anaesthetic to their theological and political enthusiasms. He finds himself an alien at their feasts of soul. And so he withdraws into his tower, and is heard of no more. Cabell is almost a perfect example. His eyes, for years, were turned toward the past; he became a professor of the grotesque genealogizing that decaying aristocracies affect; it was only by a sort of accident that he discovered himself to be an artist. The south is unaware of the fact to this day; it regards Woodrow Wilson and Col. John Temple Graves as much finer stylists, and Frank L. Stanton as an infinitely greater poet. If it has heard, which I doubt, that Cabell has been hoofed by the Comstocks, it unquestionably views that assault as a deserved rebuke to a fellow who indulges a lewd passion for fancy writing, and is a covert enemy to the Only True Christianity.

What is needed down there, before the vexatious public problems of the region may be intelligently approached, is a survey of the population by competent ethnologists and anthropologists. The immigrants of the north have been studied at great length, and any one who is interested may now apply to the Bureau of Ethnology for elaborate data as to their racial strains, their stature and cranial indices, their relative capacity for education, and the changes that they undergo under American Kultur. But the older stocks of the south, and particularly the emancipated and dominant poor white trash, have never been investigated scientifically, and most of the current generalizations about them are probably wrong. For example, the generalization that they are purely Anglo-Saxon in blood. This I doubt very seriously. The chief strain down there, I believe, is Celtic rather than Saxon, particularly in the hill country. French blood, too, shows itself here and there, and so does Spanish, and so does German. The last-named entered from the northward, by way of the limestone belt just east of the Alleghenies. Again, it is very likely that in some parts of the south a good many of the plebeian whites have more than a trace of negro blood. Interbreeding under concubinage produced some very light half-breeds at an early day, and no doubt appreciable numbers of them wit over into the white race by the simple process of changing their abode. Not long ago I read a curious article by an intelligent negro, in which he stated that it is easy for a very light negro to pass as white in the south on account of the fact that large numbers of southerners accepted as white have distinctly negroid features. Thus it becomes a delicate and dangerous matter for a train conductor or a hotel-keeper to challenge a suspect. But the Celtic strain is far more obvious than any of these others. It not only makes itself visible in physical stigmata — e. g., leanness and dark coloring — but also in mental traits. For example, the religious thought of the south is almost precisely identical with the religious thought of Wales. There is the same naive belief in an anthropomorphic Creator but little removed, in manner and desire, from an evangelical bishop; there is the same submission to an ignorant and impudent sacerdotal tyranny, and there is the same sharp contrast between doctrinal orthodoxy and private ethics. Read Caradoc Evans' ironical picture of the Welsh Wesleyans in his preface to "My Neighbors," and you will be instantly reminded of the Georgia and Carolina Methodists. The most booming sort of piety, in the south, is not incompatible with the theory that lynching is a benign institution. Two generations ago it was not incompatible with an ardent belief in slavery.

It is highly probable that some of the worst blood of western Europe flows in the veins of the southern poor whites, now poor no longer. The original strains, according to every honest historian, were extremely corrupt. Philip Alexander Bruce (a Virginian of the old gentry) says in his "Industrial History of Virginia in the Seventeenth Century" that the first native-born generation was largely illegitimate. "One of the most common offenses against morality committed in the lower ranks of life in Virginia during the seventeenth century," he says, "was bastardy." The mothers of these bastards, he continues, were chiefly indentured servants, and "had belonged to the lowest class in their native country." Fanny Kernble Butler, writing of the Georgia poor whites of a century later, described them as "the most degraded race of human beings claiming an Anglo-Saxon origin that can be found on the face of the earth — filthy, lazy, ignorant, brutal, proud, penniless savages." The Sunday-school and the chautauqua, of course, have appreciably mellowed the descendants of these "savages," and their economic progress and rise to political power have done perhaps even more, but the marks of their origin are still unpleasantly plentiful. Every now and then they produce a political leader who puts their secret notions of the true, the good and the beautiful into plain words, to the amazement and scandal of the rest of the country. That amazement is turned into downright incredulity when news comes that his platform has got him high office, and that he is trying to execute it.

In the great days of the south the line between the gentry and the poor whites was very sharply drawn. There was absolutely no intermarriage. So far as I know there is not a single instance in history of a southerner of the upper class marrying one of the bondwomen described by Mr. Bruce. In other societies characterized by class distinctions of that sort it is common for the lower class to be improved by extra-legal crosses. That is to say, the men of the upper class take women of the lower class as mistresses, and out of such unions spring the extraordinary plebeians who rise sharply from the common level, and so propagate the delusion that all other plebeians would do the same thing if they had the chance — in brief, the delusion that class distinctions are merely economic and conventional, and not congenital and genuine. But in the south the men of the upper classes sought their mistresses among the blacks, and after a few generations there was so much white blood in the black women that they were considerably more attractive than the unhealthy and bedraggled women of the poor whites. This preference continued into our own time. A southerner of good family once told me in all seriousness that he had reached his majority before it ever occurred to him that a white woman might make quite as agreeable a mistress as the octaroons of his jejune fancy. If the thing has changed of late, it is not the fault of the southern white man, but of the southern mulatto women. The more slightly yellow girls of the region, with improving economic opportunities, have gained self-respect, and so they are no longer as willing to enter into concubinage as their grand-dams were.

As a result of this preference of the southern gentry for mulatto mistresses there was created a series of mixed strains containing the best white blood of the south, and perhaps of the whole country. As another result the poor whites went unfertilized from above, and so missed the improvement that so constantly shows itself in the peasant stocks of other countries. It is a commonplace that nearly all negroes who rise above the general are of mixed blood, usually with the white predominating. I know a great many negroes, and it would be hard for me to think of an exception. What is too often forgotten is that this white blood is not the blood of the poor whites but that of the old gentry. The mulatto girls of the early days despised the poor whites as creatures distinctly inferior to negroes, and it was thus almost unheard of for such a girl to enter into relations with a man of that submerged class. This aversion was based upon a sound instinct. The southern mulatto of to-day is a proof of it. Like all other half-breeds he is an unhappy man, with disquieting tendencies toward anti-social habits of thought, but he is intrinsically a better animal than the pure-blooded descendant of the old poor whites, and he not infrequently demonstrates it. It is not by accident that the negroes of the south are making faster progress, economically and culturally, than the masses of the whites. It is not by accident that the only visible aesthetic activity in the south is wholly in their hands. No southern composer has ever written music so good as that of half a dozen white-black composers who might be named. Even in politics, the negro reveals a curious superiority. Despite the fact that the race question has been the main political concern of the southern whites for two generations, to the practical exclusion of everything else, they have contributed nothing to its discussion that has impressed the rest of the world so deeply and so favorably as three or four books by southern negroes.

Entering upon such themes, of course, one must resign one's self to a vast misunderstanding and abuse. The south has not only lost its old capacity for producing ideas; it has also taken on the worst intolerance of ignorance and stupidity. Its prevailing mental attitude for several decades past has been that of its own hedge ecclesiastics. All who dissent from its orthodox doctrines are scoundrels. All who presume to discuss its ways realistically are damned. I have had, in my day, several experiences in point. Once, after I had published an article on some phase of the eternal race question, a leading southern newspaper replied by printing a column of denunciation of my father, then dead nearly twenty years — a philippic placarding him as an ignorant foreigner of dubious origin, inhabiting "The Baltimore ghetto" and speaking a dialect recalling that of Weber & Fields — two thousand words of incandescent nonsense, utterly false and beside the point, but exactly meeting the latter-day southern notion of effective controversy. Another time, I published a short discourse on lynching, arguing that the sport was popular in the south because the backward culture of the region denied the populace more seemly recreations. Among such recreations I m"xtioned those afforded by brass bands, symphony orchestras, boxing matches, amateur athletic contests, shoot-the-chutes, roof gardens, horse races, and so on. In reply another great southern journal denounced me as a man 'of wineshop temperament, brass-jewelry tastes and pornographic predilections." In other words, brass bands, in the south, are classed with brass jewelry, and both are snares of the devil! To advocate setting up symphony orchestras is pornography! . . . Alas, when the touchy southerner attempts a greater urbanity, the result is often even worse. Some time ago a colleague of mine printed an article deploring the arrested cultural development of Georgia. In reply he received a number of protests from patriotic Georgians, and all of them solemnly listed the glories of the state. I indulge in a few specimens:

Who has not heard of Asa G. Candler, whose name is synonymous with Coca-Cola, a Georgia product?

The first Sunday-school in the world was opened in Savannah.

Who does not recall with pleasure the writings of Frank L. Stanton, Georgia's brilliant poet?

Georgia was the first state to organize a Boys' Corn Club in the South — Newton county, 1904.

The first to suggest a common United Daughters of the Confederacy badge was Mrs. Raynes, of Georgia.

The first to suggest a state historian of the United Daughters of the Confederacy was Mrs. C. Helen Plane (Macon convention, 1896).

The first to suggest putting to music Heber's "From Greenland's Icy Mountains" was Mrs. F. R. Goulding, of Savannah.

And so on, and so on. These proud boasts came, remember, not from obscure private persons, but from "Leading Georgians" — in one case, the state historian. Curious sidelights upon the ex-Confederate mind! Another comes from a stray copy of a negro paper. It describes an ordinance lately passed by the city council of Douglas, Ga., forbidding any trousers presser, on penalty of forfeiting a $500 bond, to engage in "pressing for both white and colored." This in a town, says the negro paper, where practically all of the white inhabitants have "their food prepared by colored hands," "their babies cared for by colored hands," and "the clothes which they wear right next to their skins washed in houses where negroes live" — houses in which the said clothes "remain for as long as a week at a time." But if you marvel at the absurdity, keep it dark! A casual word, and the united press of the south will be upon your trail, denouncing you bitterly as a scoundrelly Yankee, a Bolshevik Jew, an agent of the Wilhelmstrasse.. • •

Obviously, it is impossible for intelligence to flourish in such an atmosphere. Free inquiry is blocked by the idiotic certainties of ignorant men. The arts, save in the lower reaches of the gospel hymn, the phonograph and the chautauqua harangue, are all held in suspicion. The tone of public opinion is set by an upstart class but lately emerged from industrial slavery into commercial enterprise — the class of "hustling" business men, of "live wires," of commercial club luminaries, of 'drive" managers, of forward-lookers and right-thinkers — in brief, of third rate southerners inoculated with all the worst traits of the Yankee sharper. One observes the curious effects of an old tradition of truculence upon a population now merely pushful and impudent, of an old tradition of chivalry upon a population now quite without imagination. The old repose is gone. The old romanticism is gone. The philistinism of the new type of town-boomer southerner is not only indifferent to the ideals of the old south; it is positively antagonistic to them. That philistinism regards human life, not as an agreeable adventure, but as a mere trial of rectitude and efficiency. It is overwhelmingly utilitarian and moral. It is inconceivably hollow and obnoxious. What remains of the ancient tradition is simply a certain charming civility in private inter- course—often broken down, alas, by the hot rages of Puritanism, but still generally visible. The south- erner, at his worst, is never quite the surly cad that the Yankee is. His sensitiveness may betray him into occasional bad manners, but in the main he is a pleasant fellow—hospitable, polite, good-humored, even jovial. . . . But a bit absurd. ... A bit pathetic.

IV. THE DIVINE AFFLATUS

THE suave and (edematous Chesterton, in a late effort to earn the honorarium of a Chicago newspaper, composed a thousand words of labored counterblast to what is called inspiration in the arts. The thing itself, he argued, has little if any actual existence; we hear so much about it because its alleged coyness and fortuitousness offer a convenient apology for third-rate work. The man taken in such third-rate work excuses himself on the ground that he is a helpless slave of some power that stands outside him, and is quite beyond his control. On days when it favors him he teems with ideas and creates masterpieces, but on days when it neglects him he is crippled and impotent — a fiddle without a bow, an engine without steam, a tire without air. All this, according to Chesterton, is nonsense. A man who can really write at all, or paint at all, or compose at all should be able to do it at almost any time, provided only "he is not drunk or asleep."

So far Chesterton. The formula of the argument is simple and familiar: to dispose of a problem all that is necessary is to deny that it exists. But there are plenty of men, I believe, who find themselves unable to resolve the difficulty in any such cavalier manner — men whose chief burden and distinction, in fact, is that they do not employ formulae in their thinking, but are thrown constantly upon industry, ingenuity and the favor of God. Among such men there remains a good deal more belief in what is vaguely called inspiration. They know by hard experience that there are days when their ideas flow freely and clearly, and days when they are dammed up damnably. Say a man of that sort has a good day. For some reason quite incomprehensible to him all his mental processes take on an amazing ease and slickness. Almost without conscious effort he solves technical problems that have badgered him for weeks. He is full of novel expedients, extraordinary efficiencies, strange cunnings. He has a feeling that he has suddenly and unaccountably broken through a wall, dispersed a fog, got himself out of the dark. So he does a double or triple stint of the best work that he is capable of — maybe of far better work than he has ever been capable of before — and goes to bed impatient for the morrow. And on the morrow he discovers to his consternation that he has become almost idiotic, and quite incapable of any work at all.

I challenge any man who trades in ideas to deny that he has this experience. The truth is that he has it constantly. It overtakes poets and contrapuntists, critics and dramatists, philosophers and journalists; it may even be shared, so far as I know, by advertisement writers, chautauqua orators and the rev. clergy. The characters that all anatomists of melancholy mark in it are the irregular ebb and flow of the tides, and the impossibility of getting them under any sort of rational control. The brain, as it were, stands to one side and watches itself pitching and tossing, full of agony but essentially helpless. Here the man of creative imagination pays a ghastly price for all his superiorities and immunities; nature takes revenge upon him for dreaming of improvements in the scheme of things. Sitting there in his lonely room, gnawing the handle of his pen, racked by his infernal quest, horribly bedevilled by incessant flashes of itching, toothache, eye-strain and evil conscience — thus tortured, he makes atonement for his crime of being intelligent. The normal man, the healthy and honest man, the good citizen and householder — this man, I daresay, knows nothing of all that travail. It is reserved especially for artists and metaphysicians. It is the particular penalty of those who pursue strange butterflies into dark forests, and go fishing in enchanted and forbidden streams.

Let us, then, assume that the fact is proved: the nearest poet is a witness to it. But what of the underlying mystery? How are we to account for that puckish and inexplicable rise and fall of inspiration?

My questions, of course, are purely rhetorical. Explanations exist; they have existed for all time; there is always a well-known solution to every human problem—neat, plausible, and wrong. The ancients, in the case at bar, laid the blame upon the gods: sometimes they were remote and surly, and sometimes they were kind. In the Middle Ages lesser powers took a hand in the matter, and so one reads of works of art inspired by Our Lady, by the Blessed Saints, by the souls of the departed, and even by the devil. In our own day there are explanations less super- natural but no less fanciful—to wit, the explanation that the whole thing is a matter of pure chance, and not to be resolved into any orderly process—to wit, the explanation that the controlling factor is external circumstance, that the artist happily married to a dutiful wife is thereby inspired—finally, to make an end, the explanation that it is all a question of Freudian complexes, themselves lurking in impenetrable shadows. But all of these explanations fail to satisfy the mind that is not to be put off with mere words. Some of them are palpably absurd; others beg the question. The problem of the how remains, even when the problem of the why is disposed of. What is the precise machinery whereby the cerebrum is bestirred to such abnormal activity on one day that it sparkles and splutters like an arclight, and reduced to such feebleness on another day that it smokes and gutters like a tallow dip? In this emergency, having regard for the ages-long and unrelieved sufferings of artists great and small, I offer a new, simple, and at all events not ghostly solution. It is supported by the observed facts, by logical analogies and by the soundest known principles of psychology, and so I present it without apologies. It may be couched, for convenience, in the following brief terms: that inspiration, so-called, is a function of metabolism, and that it is chiefly conditioned by the state of the intestinal flora—in larger words, that a man's flow of ideas is controlled and determined, both quantitatively and qualitatively, not by the whims of the gods, nor by the terms of his armistice with his wife, nor by the combinations of some transcendental set of dice, but by the chemical content of the blood that lifts itself from his liver to his brain, and that this chemical content is established in his digestive tract, particularly south of the pylorus. A man may write great poetry when he is drunk, when he is cold and miserable, when he is bankrupt, when he has a black eye, when his wife glowers at him across the table, when his children lie dying of smallpox; he may even write it during an earthquake, or while crossing the English channel, or in the midst of a Methodist revival, or in New York. But I am so far gone in materialism that I am disposed to deny flatly and finally, and herewith do deny flatly and finally, that there has lived a poet in the whole history of the world, ancient or modern, near or far, who ever managed to write great poetry, or even passably fair and decent poetry, at a time when he was suffering from stenosis at any point along the thirty-foot via dolorosa running from the pylorus to the sigmoid flexure. In other words, when he was —

But perhaps I had better leave your medical adviser to explain. After all, it is not necessary to go any further in this direction; the whole thing may be argued in terms of the blood stream — and the blood stream is respectable, as the duodenum is an outcast It is the blood and the blood only, in fact, that the cerebrum is aware of; of what goes on elsewhere it can learn only by hearsay. If all is well below, then the blood that enters the brain through the internal carotid is full of the elements necessary to bestir the brain-cells to their highest activity; if, on the contrary, anabolism and katabolism are going on ineptly, if the blood is not getting the supplies that it needs and not getting rid of the wastes that burden it, then the braincells will be both starved and poisoned, and not all the king's horses and all the king's men can make them do their work with any show of ease and efficiency. In the first case the man whose psyche dwells in the cells will have a moment of inspiration — that is, he will find it a strangely simple and facile matter to write his poem, or iron out his syllogism, or make his bold modulation from F sharp minor to C major, or get his flesh-tone, or maybe only perfect his swindle. But in the second case he will be stumped and helpless. The more he tries, the more vividly he will be conscious of his impotence. Sweat will stand out in beads upon his brow, he will fish patiently for the elusive thought, he will try coaxing and subterfuge, he will retire to his ivory tower, he will tempt the invisible powers with black coffee, tea, alcohol and the alkaloids, he may even curse Cod and invite death — but he will not write his poem, or iron out his syllogism, or find his way into C major, or get his flesh-tone, or perfect his swindle.

Fix your eye upon this hypothesis of metabolic inspiration, and at once you will find the key to many a correlative mystery. For one thing, it quickly explains the observed hopelessness of trying to pump up inspiration by mere hard industry — the essential imbecility of the 1,000 words a day formula. Let there be stenosis below, and not all the industry of a Hercules will suffice to awaken the lethargic brain. Here, indeed, the harder the striving, the worse the stagnation — as every artist knows only too well. And why not? Striving in the face of such an interior obstacle is the most cruel of enterprises — a business more nerve-wracking and exhausting than reading a newspaper or watching a bad play. The pain thus produced, the emotions thus engendered, react upon the liver in a manner scientifically displayed by Dr. George W. Crile in his "Man: An Adaptive Mechanism," and the result is a steady increase in the intestinal demoralization, and a like increase in the pollution of the blood. In the had the poor victim comes to a familiar pass; beset on the one hand by impotence and on the other hand by an impatience grown pathological, he gets into a state indistinguishable from the frantic. It is at such times that creative artists suffer most atrociously. It is then that they writhe upon the sharp spears and red-hot hooks of a jealous and unjust Creator for their invasion of His monopoly. It is then that they pay a grisly supertax upon their superiority to the great herd of law-abiding and undistinguished men. The men of this herd never undergo any comparable torture; the agony of the artist is quite beyond their experience and even beyond their imagination. No catastrophe that could conceivably overtake a lime and cement dealer, a curb broker, a lawyer, a plumber or a Presbyterian is to be mentioned in the same breath with the torments that, to the most minor of poets, are familiar incidents of his professional life, and, to such a man as Poe, or Beethoven, or Brahms, are the commonplaces of every day. Beethoven suffered more during the composition of the Fifth symphony than all the judges on the supreme benches of the world have suffered jointly since the time of the Gerousia.

Again, my hypothesis explains the fact that inspiration, save under extraordinary circumstances, is never continuous for more than a relatively short period. A banker, a barber or a manufacturer of patent medicines does his work day after day without any noticeable rise or fall of efficiency; save when he is drunk, jailed or ill in bed the curve of his achievement is flattened out until it becomes almost a straight line. But the curve of an artist, even of the greatest of artists, is frightfully zig-zagged. There are moments when it sinks below the bottom of the chart, and immediately following there may be moments when it threatens to run off the top. Some of the noblest passages written by Shakespeare are in his worst plays, cheek by jowl with padding and banality; some of the worst music of Wagner is in his finest music dramas. There is, indeed, no such thing as a flawless masterpiece. Long labored, it may be gradually enriched with purple passages — the high inspirations of widely separated times crowded together — but even so it will remain spotty, for those purple passages will be clumsily joined, and their joints will remain as apparent as so many false teeth. Only the most elementary knowledge of psychology is needed to show the cause of the zig-zagging that I have mentioned. It lies in the elemental fact that the chemical constitution of the blood changes every hour, almost every minute. What it is at the beginning of digestion is not what it is at the end of digestion, and in both cases it is enormously affected by the nature of the substances digested. No man, within twenty-four hours after eating a meal in a Pennsylvania Railroad dining-car, could conceivably write anything worth reading. A tough beefsteak, I daresay, has ditched many a promising sonnet, and bad beer, as every one knows, has spoiled hundreds of sonatas. Thus inspiration rises and falls, and even when it rises twice to the same height it usually shows some qualitative difference — there is the inspiration, say, of Spring vegetables and there is the inspiration of Autumn fruits. In a long work the products of greatly differing inspirations, of greatly differing streams of blood, are hideously intermingled, and the result is the inevitable spottiness that I have mentioned. No one but a maniac argues that "Die Meistersinger" is all good. One detects in it days when Wagner felt, as the saying goes, like a fighting cock, but one also detects days when he arose in the morning full of acidosis and despair — days when he turned heavily from the Pierian spring to castor oil.

Moreover, it must be obvious that the very conditions under which works of art are produced tend to cause great aberrations in metabolism. The artist is forced by his calling to be a sedentary man. Even a poet, perhaps the freest of artists, must spend a good deal of time bending over a desk. He may conceive his poems in the open air, as Beethoven conceived his music, but the work of reducing them to actual words requires diligent effort in camera. Here it is a sheer impossibility for him to enjoy the ideal hygienic conditions which surround the farmhand, the curb-broker and the sailor. His viscera are congested; his eyes are astrain; his muscles are without necessary exercise. Furthermore, he probably breathes bad air and goes without needed sleep. The result is inevitably some disturbance of metabolism, with a vitiated blood supply and a starved cerebrum. One is always surprised to encounter a poet who is ruddy and stout; the standard model is a pale and flabby stenotic, kept alive by patent medicines. So with the painter, the musical composer, the sculptor, the artist in prose. There is no more confining work known to man than instrumentation. The composer who has spent a day at it is invariably nervous and ill. For hours his body is bent over his music-paper, the while his pen engrosses little dots upon thin lines. I have known composers, after a week or so of such labor, to come down with auto-intoxication in its most virulent forms. Perhaps the notorious ill health of Beethoven, and the mental break-downs of Schumann, Tschaikowsky and Hugo Wolf had their origin in this direction. It is difficult, going through the history of music, to find a single composer in the grand manner who was physically and mentally up to pan

I do not advance it as a formal corollary, but no doubt this stenosis hypothesis also throws some light upon two other immemorial mysteries, the first being the relative aesthetic sterility of women, and the other being the low aesthetic development of certain whole classes, and even races of men, e. g., the Puritans, the Welsh and the Confederate Americans. That women suffer from stenosis far more than men is a commonplace of internal medicine; the weakness is chiefly to blame, rather than the functional peculiarities that they accuse, for their liability to headache. A good many of them, in fact, are habitually in the state of health which, in the artist, is accompanied by an utter inability to work. This state of health, as I have said, does not inhibit all mental activity. It leaves the powers of observation but little impaired; it does not corrupt common sense; it is not incompatible with an intelligent discharge of the ordinary duties of life. Thus a lime and cement dealer, in the midst of it, may function almost as well as when his metabolic processes are perfectly normal, and by the same token a woman chronically a victim to it may yet show all the sharp mental competence which characterizes her sex. But here the thing stops. To go beyond — to enter the realm of constructive thinking, to abandon the mere application of old ideas and essay to invent new ideas, to precipitate novel and intellectual concepts out of the chaos of memory and perception — this is quite

66

impossible to the stenotic. Ergo, it is unheard of among classics and races of men who feed grossly and neglect personal hygiene; the pill-swallower is the only artist in such groups. One may thus argue that the elder Beecham saved poetry in England, as the younger Beecham saved music. . . . But, as I say, I do not stand behind the hypothesis in this department, save, perhaps, in the matter of women. I could amass enormous evidences in favor of it, but against them there would always loom the disconcerting contrary evidence of the Bulgarians. Among them, I suppose, stenosis must be unknown — but so are all the fine arts. "La force et la foiblesse de Tesprit," said Rochefoucauld, "sont mal nommees; elles ne sont, en effect, que la bonne ou la mauvaise des organes du corps." Science wastes itself hunting in the other direction. We are flooded with evidences of the effects of the mind on the body, and so our attention is diverted from the enormously greater effects of the body on the mind. It is rather astonishing that the Wassermann reaction has not caused the latter to be investigated more thoroughly. The first result of the general employment of that great diagnostic device was the discovery that thousands of cases of so-called mental disease were really purely physical in origin — that thousands of patients long supposed to have been crazed by seeing ghosts, by love, by grief, or by reverses in the stock-market were actually victims of the small but extremely enterprising spirochaete pallida. The news heaved a bomb into psychiatry, but it has so far failed to provoke a study of the effects of other such physical agents. Even the effects of this one agent remain to be inquired into at length. One now knows that it may cause insanity, but what of the lesser mental aberrations that it produces? Some of these aberrations may be actually beneficial. That is to say, the mild toxemia accompanying the less virulent forms of infection may stimulate the brain to its highest functioning, and so give birth to what is called genius — a state of mind long recognized, by popular empiricism, as a sort of half-way station on the road to insanity. Beethoven, Nietzsche and Schopenhauer suffered from such mild toxemias, and there is not the slightest doubt that their extraordinary mental activity was at least partly due to the fact. That tuberculosis, in its early stages, is capable of the same stimulation is a commonplace of observation. The consumptive may be weak physically, but he is usually very alert mentally. The history of the arts, in fact, shows the names of hundreds of inspired consumptives.

Here a physical infirmity produces a result that is beneficial, just as another physical infirmity, the stenosis aforesaid, produces a result that is baleful. The artist often oscillates horribly between the two effects; he is normally anything but a healthy animal. Perfect health, indeed, is a boon that very few men above the rank of clodhoppers ever enjoy. What health means is a degree of adaptation to the organism's environment so nearly complete that there is no irritation. Such a state, it must be obvious, is not often to be observed in organisms of the highest complexity. It is common, perhaps, in the earthworm. This elemental beast makes few demands upon its environment, and is thus subject to few diseases. It seldom gets out of order until the sands of its life are run, and then it suffers one grand illness and dies forthwith. But man is forever getting out of order, for he is enormously complicated — and the higher he rises in complexity, the more numerous and the more serious are his derangements. There are whole categories of diseases, e. g., neurasthenia and hay-fever, that afflict chiefly the more civilized and delicate ranks of men, leaving the inferior orders unscathed. Good health in man, indeed, is almost invariably a function of inferiority. A professionally healthy man, e. g., an acrobat, an osteopath or an ice-wagon driver, is always stupid. In the Greece of the great days the athletes we hear so much about were mainly slaves. Not one of the eminent philosophers, poets or statesmen of Greece was a good high-jumper. Nearly all of them, in fact, suffered from the same malaises which afflict their successors of to-day, as you will quickly discern by examining their compositions. The aesthetic impulse, like the thirst for truth, might almost be called a disease. It seldom if ever appears in a perfectly healthy man.

But we must take the aloes with the honey. The artist suffers damnably, but there is compensation in his dreams. Some of his characteristic diseases cripple him and make his whole life a misery, but there are others that seem to help him. Of the latter, the two that I have mentioned carry with them concepts of extreme obnoxiousness. Both are infections, and one is associated in the popular mind with notions or gross immorality. But these concepts of obnoxiousness should not blind us to the benefits that apparently go with the maladies. There are, in fact, maladies much more obnoxious, and they carry no compensating benefits. Cancer is an example. Perhaps the time will come when the precise effects of these diseases will be worked out accurately, and it will be possible to gauge in advance their probable influence upon this or that individual. If that time ever comes the manufacture of artists will become a feasible procedure, like the present manufacture of soldiers, capons, right-thinkers and doctors of philosophy. In those days the promising young men of the race, instead of being protected from such diseases at all hazards, will be deliberately infected with them, as soils are now inoculated with nitrogen-liberating bacteria.... At the same time, let us hope, some progress will be made against stenosis. It is, after all, simply a question of technique, like the artificial propagation of the race by the device of Dr. Jacques Loeb. The poet of the future, come upon a period of doldrums, will not tear his hair in futile agony. Instead, he will go to the nearest clinic, and there get his rasher of Bulgarian bacilli, or an injection of some complex organic compound out of a ductless gland, or an order on a masseur, or a diet list, or perchance a barrel of Russian oil.

V. SCIENTIFIC EXAMINATION OF A POPULAR VIRTUE

AN old Corpsbruder, assaulting my ear lately with an abstruse tale of his sister's husband's brother's ingratitude, ended by driving me quite out of his house, firmly resolved to be his acquaintance no longer. The exact offense I heard inattentively, and have already partly forgotten— an obscure tort arising out of a lawsuit. My ex- friend, it appears, was appealed to for help in a bad case by his grapevine relative, and so went on the stand for him and swore gallantly to some complex and unintelligible lie. Later on, essaying to cash in on the perjury, he asked the fellow to aid him in some domestic unpleasantness, and was refused on grounds of morals. Hence his indignation—and my spoiled evening. ... What is one to think of a man so asinine that he looks for gratitude in this world, or so puerilely egotistical that he enjoys it when found? The truth is that the sentiment itself is not human but doggish, and that the man who demands it in payment for his doings is precisely the sort of man who feels noble and distinguished when a dog licks his hand. What a man says when he expresses gratitude is simply this: "You did something for me that I could not have done myself. Ergo, you are my superior. Hail, Durchlaucht!" Such a confession, whether true or not, is degrading to the confessor, and so it is very hard to make, at all events for a man of self-respect. That is why such a man always makes it clumsily and with many blushes and hesitations. It is hard for him to put so embarrassing a doctrine into plain words. And that is why the business is equally uncomfortable to the party of the other part. It distresses him to see a human being of decent instincts standing before him in so ignominious a position. He is as flustered as if the fellow came in handcuffs, or in rags, or wearing the stripes of a felon.

Moreover, his confusion is helped out by his inward knowledge —very clear if he is introspective, and plain enough even if he is not—that he really deserves no such tribute to his high mightiness; that the altruism for which he is being praised was really bogus; that he did the thing behind the gratitude which now assails him, not for any grand and lofty reason, but for a purely selfish and inferior reason, to wit, for the reason that it pleases all of us to show what we can do when an appreciative audience is present; that we delight to exercise our will to power when it is safe and profitable. This is the primary cause of the benefits which inspire gratitude, real and pretended. This is the fact at the bottom of altruism. Find me a man who is always doing favors for people and I will show you a man of petty vanity, forever trying to get fuel for it in the cheapest way. And find me a man who is notoriously grateful in habit and I'll show you a man who is essentially third rate and who is conscious of it at the bottom of his heart. The man of genuine self-respect — which means the man who is more or less accurately aware, not only of his own value, but also and more importantly, of his own limitations — tries to avoid entering either class.

He hesitates to demonstrate his superiority by such banal means, and he shrinks from confessing an inferiority that he doesn't believe in.

Nevertheless, the popular morality of the world, which is the creation, not of its superior men but of its botches and half -men — in brief, of its majorities — puts a high value on gratitude and denounces the withholding of it as an offense against the proprieties. To be noticeably ungrateful for benefits — that is, for the by-products of the egotism of others — is to be disliked. To tell a tale of ingratitude is to take on the aspect of a martyr to the defects of others, to get sympathy in an affliction. All of us are responsive to such ideas, however much we may resent them logically. One may no more live in the world without picking up the moral prejudices of the world than one will be able to go to hell without perspiring. ...

Let me recall a case within my own recent experience. One day I received a letter from a young woman I had never heard of before, asking me to read the manuscripts of two novels that she had written. She represented that she had venerated my critical parts for a long while, and that her whole future career in letters would be determined by my decision as to her talents. The daughter of a man apparently of some consequence in some sordid business or other, she asked me to meet her at her father's office, and there to impart to her, under socially aseptic conditions, my advice. Having a standing rule against meeting women authors, even in their fathers' banks and soap factories, I pleaded various imaginary engagements, but finally agreed, after a telephone debate, to read her manuscripts. They arrived promptly and I found them to be wholly without merit — in fact, the veriest twaddle. Nevertheless I plowed through them diligently, wasted half an hour at the job, wrote a polite letter of counsel and returned the manuscripts to her house, paying a blackamoor 50 cents to haul them.

By all ordinary standards, an altruistic service and well deserving some show of gratitude. Had she knitted me a pair of pulse-warmers it would have seemed meet and proper. Even a copy of the poems of Alfred Noyes would not have been too much. At the very least I expected a note of thanks. Well, not a word has ever reached me. For all my laborious politeness and disagreeable labor my reward is exactly nil. The lady is improved by my counsel — and I am shocked by her gross ingratitude. . . That is, conventionally, superficially, as a member of society in good standing. But when on sour afternoons I roll the affair in my mind, examining, not the mere surface of it but the inner workings and anatomy of it, my sense of outrage gradually melts and fades away — the inevitable recompense of skepticism. What I see clearly is that I was an ass to succumb to the blandishments of this discourteous miss, and that she was quite right in estimating my service trivially, and out of that clear seeing comes consolation, and amusement, and, in the end, even satisfaction. I got exactly what I deserved. And she, whether consciously or merely instinctively, measured out the dose with excellent accuracy.

Let us go back. Why did I waste two hours, or maybe three, reading those idiotic manuscripts? Why, in the first place, did I answer her opening request — the request, so inherently absurd, that I meet her in her father's office? For a very plain reason: she accompanied it with flattery. What she said, in effect, was that she regarded me as a critic of the highest talents, and this ludicrous cajolery — sound, I dare say, in substance, but reduced to naught by her obvious obscurity and stupidity — wag quite enough to fetch me. In brief, she assumed that, being a man, I was vain to the point of imbecility, and this assumption was correct, as it always is. To help out, there was the concept of romantic adventure vaguely floating in my mind. Her voice, as I heard it by telephone, was agreeable; her appearance, since she seemed eager to show herself, I probably judged (subconsciously) to be at least not revolting. Thus curiosity got on its legs, and vanity in another form. Am I fat and half decrepit, a man seldom noticed by cuties? Then so much the more reason why I should respond. The novelty of an apparently comely and respectable woman desiring to witness me finished what the primary (and very crude) appeal to my vanity had begun. I was, in brief, not only the literary popinjay but also the eternal male — and hard at the immemorial folly of the order.

Now turn to the gal and her ingratitude. The more I inspect it the more I became convinced that it is not discreditable to her, but highly creditable — that she demonstrates a certain human dignity, despite her imbecile writings, by exhibiting it. Would a show of gratitude put her in a better light? I doubt it. That gratitude, considering the unfavorable report I made on her manuscripts, would be doubly invasive of her amour propre. On the one hand it would involve a confession that my opinion of her literary gifts was better than her own, and that I was thus her superior. And on the other hand it would involve a confession that my own actual writings (being got into print without aid) were better than hers, and that I was thus her superior again. Each confession would bring her into an attitude of abasement, and the two together would make her position intolerable. Moreover, both would be dishonest: she would privately believe in neither doctrine. As for my opinion, its hostility to her aspiration is obviously enough to make her ego dismiss it as false, for no organism acquiesces in its own destruction. And as for my relative worth as a literary artist, she must inevitably put it very low, for it depends, in the last analysis, upon my dignity and sagacity as a man, and she has proved by experiment, and quite easily, that I am almost as susceptible to flattery as a moving picture actor, and hence surely no great shakes.

Thus there is not the slightest reason in the world why the fair creature should knit me a pair of pulse-warmers or send me the poems of Noyes, or even write me a polite note. If she did any of these things, she would feel herself a hypocrite and hence stand embarrassed before the mirror of her own thoughts.

Confronted by a choice between this sort of shame and the incomparably less uncomfortable shame of violating a social convention and an article of popular morals, secretly and without danger of exposure, she very sensibly chooses the more innocuous of the two.

At the very start, indeed, she set up barriers against gratitude, for her decision to ask a favor of me was, in a subtle sense, a judgment of my inferiority. One does not ask favors, if it can be avoided, of persons one genuinely respects; one puts such burdens upon the naive and colorless, upon what are called the good natured; in brief, upon one's inferiors. When that girl first thought of me as a possible aid to her literary aspiration she thought of me (perhaps vaguely, but none the less certainly) as an inferior fortuitously outfitted with a body of puerile technical information and competence, of probable use to her. This unfavorable view was immediately reenforced by her discovery of my vanity.

In brief, she showed and still shows the great instinctive sapience of her sex. She is female, and hence far above the nonsensical delusions, vanities, conventions and moralities of men.

VI. EXEUNT OMNES

ONE of the hardest jobs that faces an magazine editor in this, the one-hundred-and forty-fifth year of the Republic, is that of keeping the minnesingers of the land from filling his magazine with lugubrious dithyrambs to, on and against somatic death. Of spiritual death, of course, not many of them ever sing. Most of them, in fact, deny its existence in plain terms; they are all sure of the immortality of the soul, and in particular they are absolutely sure of the immortality of their own souls, and of those of their best girls. In this department the most they ever allow to the materialism of the herds that lie bogged in prose is such a benefit of the half doubt as one finds in Christina Rossetti's "When I am Dead." But when it comes to somatic death, the plain brutal death of coroners' inquests and vital statistics, their optimism vanishes, and, try as they may, they can't get around the harsh fact that on such and such a day, often appallingly near, each and every one of us will heave a last sigh, roll his eyes despairingly, turn his face to the wall and then suddenly change from a proud and highly complex mammal, made in the image of God, to a mere inert aggregate of disintegrating colloids, made in the image of a stale cabbage.

The inevitability of it seems to fascinate them. They write about it more than they write about anything else save love. Every day my editorial desk is burdened with their manuscripts — poems in which the poet serves notice that, when his time comes, he will die bravely and even a bit insolently; poems in which he warns his mistress that he will wait for her on the roof of the cosmos and keep his harp in tune; poems in which he asks her grandly to forget him, and, above all, to avoid torturing herself by vain repining at his grave; poems in which he directs his heirs and assigns to bury him in some lonely, romantic spot, where the whippoorwills sing; poems in which he hints that he will not rest easily if Philistines are permitted to begaud his last anchorage with couronnes des perles; poems in which he speaks jauntily of making a rendezvous with death, as if death were a wench; poems in which —

But there is no need to rehearse the varieties. If you read the strophes that are strung along the bottoms of magazine pages you are familiar with all of them; even in the great moral periodical that I help to edit, despite my own excessive watchfulness and Dr. Nathan's general theory that both death and poetry are nuisances and in bad taste, they have appeared multitudinously, no doubt to the disgust of the intelligentsia' As I say, it is almost impossible to keep the minnesingers off the subject. When my negro flops the morning bale of poetry manuscripts upon my desk and I pull up my chair to have at them, I always make a bet with myself that, of the first dozen, at least seven will deal with death — and it is so long since I lost that I don't remember it. Periodically I send out a circular to all the recognized poets of the land, begging them in the name of God to be less mortuary, but it never does any good. More, I doubt that it ever will — or any other sort of appeal. Take away death and love and you would rob poets of both their liver and their lights; what would remain would be little more than a feeble gurgle in an illimitable void. For the business of poetry, remember, is to set up a sweet denial of the harsh facts that confront all of us — to soothe us in our agonies with emollient words — in brief, to lie sonorously and reassuringly. Well, what is the worst curse of life? Answer: the abominable magnetism that draws unlikes and incompatibles into delirious and intolerable conjunction — the kinetic over-stimulation called love. And what is the next worst? Answer: the fear of death. No wonder the poets give so much attention to both! No other foe of human peace and happiness is one-half so potent, and hence none other offers such opportunities to poetry, and, in fact, to all art. A sonnet designed to ease the dread of bankruptcy, even if done by a great master, would be banal, for that dread is itself banal, and so is bankruptcy. The same may be said of the old fear of hell, now no more. There was a day when this latter raged in the breast of nearly every man — and in that day the poets produced antidotes that were very fine poems. But to-day only the elect and anointed of God fear hell, and so there is no more production of sound poetry in that department.

As I have hinted, I tire of reading so much necrotic verse in manuscript, and wish heartily that the poets would cease to assault me with it. In prose, curiously enough, one observes a corresponding shortage. True enough, the short story of commerce shows a good many murders and suicides, and not less than eight times a day I am made privy to the agonies of a widower or widow who, on searching the papers of his wife or her husband immediately after her or his death, discovers that she or he had a lover or a mistress. But I speak of serious prose: not of trade balderdash. Go to any public library and look under "Death: Human" in the card index, and you will be surprised to find how few books there are on the subject. Worse, nearly all the few are by psychical researchers who regard death as a mere removal from one world to another or by New Thoughters who appear to believe that it is little more than a sort of illusion. Once, seeking to find out what death was physiologically — that is, to find out just what happened when a man died — I put in a solid week without result There seemed to be nothing whatever on the subject even in the medical libraries. Finally, after much weariness, I found what I was looking for in Dr. George W. Crile's "Man: An Adaptive Mechanism" — incidentally, a very solid and original work, much less heard of than it ought to be. Crile said that death was acidosis — that it was caused by the failure of the organism to maintain the alkalinity necessary to its normal functioning — and in the absence of any proofs or even arguments to the contrary I accepted his notion forthwith and have held to it ever since. I thus think of death as a sort of deleterious fermentation, like that which goes on in a bottle of Chateau Margaux when it becomes corked. Life is a struggle, not against sin, not against the Money Power, not against malicious animal magnetism, but against hydrogen ions. The healthy man is one in whom those ions, as they are dissociated by cellular activity, are immediately fixed by alkaline bases. The sick man is one in whom the process has begun to lag, with the hydrogen ions getting ahead. The dying man is one in whom it is all over save the charges of fraud. But here I get into chemical physics, and not only run afoul of revelation but also reveal, perhaps, a degree of ignorance verging upon intellectual coma.

The thing I started out to do was to call attention to the only full-length and first-rate treatise on death that I have ever encountered or heard of, to wit, "Aspects of Death and Correlated Aspects of Life," by Dr. F. Parkes Weber, a fat, hefty and extremely interesting tome, the fruit of truly stupendous erudition. What Dr. Weber has attempted is to bring together in one volume all that has been said or thought about death since the time of the first human records, not only by poets, priests and philosophers, but also by painters, engravers, soldiers, monarchs and the populace generally. The author, I take it, is primarily a numismatist, and he apparently began his work with a collection of inscriptions on coins and medals. But as it stands it covers a vastly wider area. One traces, in chapter after chapter, the ebb and flow of human ideas upon the subject, of the human attitude to the last and greatest mystery of them all — the notion of it as a mere transition to a higher plane of life, the notion of it as a benign panacea for all human suffering, the notion of it as an incentive to this or that way of living, the notion of it as an impenetrable enigma, inevitable and inexplicable. Few of us quite realize how much the contemplation of death has colored human thought throughout the ages. There have been times when it almost shut out all other concerns; there has never been a time when it has not bulked enormously in the racial consciousness.

Well, what Dr. Weber does in his hock is to detach and set forth the salient ideas that have emerged from all that consideration and discussion — to isolate the chief theories of death, ancient and modern, pagan and Christian, scientific and mystical, sound and absurd.

The material thus digested is appallingly copious. If the learned author had confined himself to printed books alone, he would have faced a labor fit for a new Hercules. But in addition to books he has given his attention to prints, to medals, to paintings, to engraved gems and to monumental inscriptions. His authorities range from St. John on what is to happen at the Day of Judgment to Sir William Osier on what happens upon the normal human death-bed, and from Socrates on the relation of death to philosophy to Havelock Ellis on the effects of Christian ideas of death upon the mediaeval temperament. The one field that Dr. Weber has overlooked is that of music" a somewhat serious omission. It is hard to think of a great composer who never wrote a funeral march, or a requiem, or at least a sad song to some departed love. Even old Papa Haydn had moments when he ceased to be merry, and let his thought turn stealthily upon the doom ahead. To me, at all events, the slow movement of the Military Symphony is the saddest of music — an elegy, I take it, on some young fellow who went out in the incomprehensible wars of those times and got himself horribly killed in a far place. The trumpet blasts towards the end fling themselves over his hasty grave in a remote cabbage field; one hears, before and after them, the honest weeping of his comrades into their wine-pots. In truth, the shadow of death hangs over all the music of Haydn, despite its lightheartedness. Life was gay in those last days of the Holy Roman Empire, but it was also precarious. If the Turks were not at the gate, then there was a peasant rising somewhere in the hinterland, or a pestilence swept the land. Beethoven, a generation later, growled at death surlily, but Haydn faced it like a gentleman. The romantic movement brought a sentimentalization of the tragedy; it became a sort of orgy. Whenever Wagner dealt with death he treated it as if it were some sort of gaudy tournament — a thing less dreadful than ecstatic. Consider, for example, the Char-Freitag music in "Parsifal" — death music for the most memorable death in the history of the world. Surely no one hearing it for the first time, without previous warning, would guess that it had to do with anything so gruesome as a crucifixion. On the contrary, I have a notion that the average auditor would guess that it was it musical setting for some lamentable fornication between a Bayreuth baritone seven feet in height and a German soprano weighing at least three hundred pounds.

But if Dr. Weber thus neglects music, he at least gives full measure in all other departments. His book, in fact, is encyclopaedic; he almost exhausts the subject. One idea, however, I do not find in it: the conception of death as the last and worst of all the practical jokes played upon poor mortals by the gods. That idea apparently never occurred to the Greeks, who thought of almost everything, but nevertheless it has an ingratiating plausibility. The hardest thing about death is not that men die tragically, but that most of them die ridiculously. If it were possible for all of us to make our exits at great moments, swiftly, cleanly, decorously, and in fine attitudes, then the experience would be something to face heroically and with high and beautiful words. But we commonly go off in no such gorgeous, poetical way. Instead, we die in raucous prose — of arterio-sclerosis, of diabetes, of toxemia, of a noisome perforation in the ileo-caecal region, of carcinoma of the liver. The abominable acidosis of Dr. Crile sneaks upon us, gradually paralyzing the adrenals, flabbergasting the thyroid, crippling the poor old liver, and throwing its fog upon the brain. Thus the ontogenetic process is recapitulated in reverse order, and we pass into the mental obscurity of infancy, and then into the blank unconsciousness of the prenatal state, and finally into the condition of undifferentiated protoplasm. A man does not die quickly and brilliantly, like a lightning stroke; he passes out by inches, hesitatingly and, one may almost add, gingerly. It is hard to say just when he is fully dead. Long after his heart has ceased to beat and his lungs have ceased to swell him up with the vanity of his species, there are remote and obscure parts of him that still live on, quite unconcerned about the central catastrophe. Dr. Alexis Carrel has cut them out and kept them alive for months. The hair keeps on growing for a long while. Every time another one of the corpses of Barbarossa or King James I is examined it is found that the hair is longer than it was the last time. No doubt there are many parts of the body, and perhaps even whole organs, which wonder what it is all about when they find that they are on the way to the crematory. Bum a man's mortal remains, and you inevitably burn a good portion of him alive, and no doubt that portion sends alarmed messages to the unconscious brain, like dissected tissue under anaesthesia, and the resultant shock brings the deceased before the hierarchy of heaven in a state of collapse, with his face white, sweat bespangling his forehead and a great thirst upon him. It would not be pulling the nose of reason to argue that many a cremated Sunday-school superintendent thus confronting the ultimate tribunal in the aspect of a man taken with the goods, has been put down as suffering from an uneasy conscience when what actually ailed him was simply surgical shock.

The cosmic process is not only incurably idiotic; it is also indecently unjust.

But here I become medico-legal. What I had in mind when I began was this: that the human tendency to make death dramatic and heroic has little excuse in the facts. No doubt you remember the scene in the last act of "'Hedda Gabler" in which Dr. Brack comes in with the news of Lovborg's suicide. Hedda immediately thinks of him putting the pistol to his temple and dying instantly and magnificently. The picture fills her with romantic delight. When Brack tells her that the shot was actually through the breast she is disappointed, but soon begins to romanticise even that. "The breast," she says, " is also a good place. . . . There is something beautiful in this!" A bit later she recurs to the charming theme, "In the breast — ah!" Then Brack tells her the plain truth — in the original, thus: "Nej,—det traf hami underlivet!" . . . Edmund Gosse, in his first English translation of the play, made the sentence: "No translation of the play, made the sentence: "No — it struck him in the abdomen." In the last edition William Archer makes it "No — in the bowels!" Abdomen is nearer to underlivet than bowels, but belly would probably raider the meaning better than either. What Brack wants to convey to Hedda is the news that Lovborg's death was not romantic in the least — that he went to a brothel, shot himself, not through the cerebrum or the heart, but through the duodenum or perhaps the jejunum, and is at the moment of report awaiting autopsy at the Christiania Allgemeine' krankenhaus. The shock floors her, but it is a shock that all of us must learn to bear. Men upon whom we lavish our veneration reduce it to an absurdity at the end by dying of chronic cystitis, or by choking upon marshmallows or dill pickles, or as the result of getting cut by dirty barbers. Women whom we place upon pedestals worthy of the holy saints come down at last with mastoid abscesses or die obscenely of hiccoughs. And we ourselves? Let us not have too much hope. The chances are that, if we go to war, eager to leap superbly at the cannon's mouth, we'll be finished on the way by an ingrowing toenail or by being run over by an army truck driven by a former Greek bus-boy and loaded with imitation Swiss cheeses made in Oneida, N. Y. And that if we die in our beds, it will be of measles or albuminuria.

The aforesaid Crile, in one of his smaller books, "A Mechanistic View of War and Peace," has a good deal to say about death in war, and in particular, about the disparity between the glorious and inspiring passing imagined by the young soldier and the messy finish that is normally in store for him. He shows two pictures of war, the one ideal and the other real. The former is the familiar print,

"The Spirit of '76," with the three patriots springing grandly to the attack, one of them with a neat and romantic bandage around his head — apparently, to judge by his liveliness, to cover a wound no worse than an average bee-sting. The latter picture is what the movie folks call a close-up of a French soldier who was struck just below the mouth by a German one-pounder shell — a soldier suddenly converted into the hideous simulacrum of a cruller. What one notices especially is the curious expression upon what remains of his face — an expression of the utmost surprise and indignation. No doubt he marched off to the front firmly convinced that, if he died at all, it would be at the climax of some heroic charge, up to his knees in blood and with his bayonet run dear through a Bavarian at least four feet in diameter. He imagined the clean bullet through the heart, the stately last gesture, the final words: Therese! Sophie! Olympe! Marie! Suzette! Odette! Denise! Julie! • . . France!" Go to the book and see what he got.

. . . Dr. Crile, whose experience of war has soured him against it, argues that the best way to abolish it would be to prohibit such romantic prints as "The Spirit of '76" and substitute therefor a series of actual photographs of dead and wounded men. The plan is plainly of merit. But it would be expensive. Imagine a war getting on its legs before the conversion of the populace had become complete. Think of the huge herds of spy-chasers, letter-openers, pacifist-hounds, burlesons and other such operators that it would take to track down and confiscate all those pictures! . . .

Even so, the vulgar horror of death would remain, for, as Ellen La Motte well says in her little book, "The Backwash of War," the finish of a civilian in a luxurious hospital, with trained nurses fluttering over him and his pastor whooping and heaving for him at the foot of his bed, is often quite as terrible as any form of exitus witnessed in war. It is, in fact, always an unpleasant business. Let the poets disguise it all they may and the theologians obscure the issue with promises of post-mortem felicity, the plain truth remains that it gives one pause to reflect that, on some day not far away, one must yield supinely to acidosis, sink into the mental darkness of an idiot, and so suffer a withdrawal from these engaging scenes. "No. 8," says the nurse in faded pink, tripping down the corridor with a hooch of rye for the diabetic in No. 2, "has just passed out." "Which is No. 8?" asks the new nurse. "The one whose wife wore that awful hat this afternoon?" . . . But all the authorities, it is pleasant to know, report that the final scene is placid enough. Dr. Weber quotes many of them. The dying man doesn't struggle much and he isn't much afraid. As his alkalies give out he succumbs to ablest stupidity. His mind fogs. His will power vanishes. He submits decently. He scarcely gives a damn.

VII. THE ALLIED ARTS

1. On Music Lovers

On Music-Lovers of all forms of the uplift, perhaps the most futile is that which addresses itself to educating the proletariat in music. The theory behind it is that a taste for music is an elevating passion, and that if the great masses of the plain people could be inoculated with it they would cease to herd into the moving-picture theaters, or to listen to Socialists, or to beat their wives and children. The defect in this theory lies in the fact that such a taste, granting it to be elevating, simply cannot be implanted. Either it is born in a man or it is not born in him. If it is, then he will get gratification for it at whatever cost— he will hear music if hell freezes over. But if it isn't, then no amount of education will ever change him— he will remain stone deaf until the last sad scene on the gallows. No child who has this congenital taste ever has to be urged or tempted or taught to love music. It takes to tone inevitably and irresistibly; nothing can restrain it. What is more, it always tries to make music, for the delight in sounds is invariably accompanied by a great desire to make them. I have never encountered an exception to this rule. All genuine music-lovers try to make music. They may do it badly, and even absurdly, but nevertheless they do it. Any man who pretends to a delight in the tone-art and yet has never learned the scale of C major — any and every such man is a fraud. The opera-houses of the world are crowded with such liars. You will even find hundreds of them in the concert-halls, though here the suffering they have to undergo to keep up their pretense is almost too much for them to bear. Many of them, true enough, deceive themselves. They are honest in the sense that they credit their own buncombe. But it is buncombe none the less.

Music, of course, has room for philanthropy. The cost of giving an orchestral concert is so great that ordinary music-lovers could not often pay for it. Here the way is open for rich backers, most of whom have no more ear for music than so many Chinamen. Nearly all the opera of the world is so supported. A few rich cads pay the bills, their wives posture obscenely in the boxes, and the genuine music-lovers upstairs and down enjoy the more or less harmonious flow of sound. But this business doesn't make musiclovers. It merely gives pleasure to music-lovers who already exist. In twenty-five years, I am sure, the

Metropolitan Opera Company hasn't converted a single music-lover. On the contrary, it has probably disgusted and alienated many thousands of fainthearted quasi-music-lovers, i. e., persons with no more than the most nebulous taste for music — so nebulous that one or two evenings of tremendous gargling by fat tenors was enough to kill it altogether.

In the United States the number of genuine musiclovers is probably very low. There are whole states, e. g., Alabama, Arkansas and Idaho, in which it would be difficult to muster a hundred. In New York, I venture, not more than one person in every thousand of the population deserves to be counted. The rest are, to all intents and purposes, tone-deaf. They can not only sit through the infernal din made by the current jazz-bands; they actually like it. This is precisely as if they preferred the works of The Duchess to those of Thomas Hardy, or the paintings of the men who make covers for popular novels to those of El Greco. Such persons inhabit the sewers of the bozart. No conceivable education could rid them of their native ignobility of soul. They are born unspeakable and incurable.

2. Opera

Opera, to a person genuinely fond of aural beauty, must inevitably appear tawdry and obnoxious, if only because it presents aural beauty in a frame of purely visual gaudiness, with overtones of the grossest sexual provocation. The most successful opera singers of the female sex, at least in America, are not those whom the majority of auditors admire most as singers but those whom the majority of male spectators desire most as mistresses. Opera is chiefly supported in all countries by the same sort of wealthy sensualists who also support musical comedy. One finds in the directors' room the traditional stock company of the stagedoor alley. Such vermin, of course, pose in the newspapers as devout and almost fanatical partisans of art; they exhibit themselves at every performance; one hears of their grand doings, through their press agents, almost every day. But one has merely to observe the sort of opera they think is good to get the measure of their actual artistic discrimination.

The genuine music-lover may accept the carnal husk of opera to get at the kernel of actual music within, but that is no sign that he approves the carnal husk or enjoys gnawing through it. Most musicians, indeed, prefer to hear operatic music outside the

opera house; that is why one so often hears such things as 'The Ride of the Valkyrie" in the concert hall. 'The Ride of the Valkyrie" has a certain intrinsic value as pure music; played by a competent orchestra it may give civilized pleasure. But as it is commonly performed in an opera house, with a posse of flat beldames throwing themselves about the stage, it can only produce the effect of a dose of ipecacuanha' The sort of person who actually delights in such spectacles is the sort of person who delights in plush furniture. Such half-wits are in a majority in every opera house west of the Rhine. They go to the opera, not to hear music, not even to hear bad music, but merely to see a more or less obscene circus. A few, perhaps, have a further purpose; they desire to assist in that circus, to show themselves in the capacity of fashionables, to enchant the yokelry with their splendor. But the majority must be content with the more lowly aim. What they get for the outrageous prices they pay for seats is a chance to feast their eyes upon glittering members of the superior demi-monde, and to abase their groveling souls before magnificoes on their own side of the footlights. They esteem a performance, not in proportion as true music is on tap, but in proportion as the display of notorious characters on the stage is copious, and the exhibition of wealth in the boxes is lavish. A soprano who can gargle her way up to G sharp in alto is more to such simple souls than a whole drove of Johann Sebastian Bachs; her one real rival, in the entire domain of art, is the contralto who has a pension from a grand duke and is reported to be enceinte by several profiteers. Heaven visualizes itself as an opera house with forty-eight Carusos, each with forty-eight press agents. • . • On the Continent, where frankness is unashamed, the opera audience often reveals its passion for tone very naively. That is to say, it arises on its hind legs, turns its back upon the stage and gapes at the boxes in charming innocence.

The music that such ignobles applaud is usually quite as shoddy as they are themselves. To write a successful opera a knowledge of harmony and counterpoint is not enough; one must also be a sort of Barnum. All the first-rate musicians who have triumphed in the opera house have been skillful mountebanks as well. I need cite only Richard Wagner and Richard Strauss. The business, indeed, has almost nothing to do with music. All the actual music one finds in many a popular opera — for example, "Thais" — mounts up to less than one may find in a pair of Cung'l waltzes. It is not this mild flavor of tone that fetches the crowd; it is the tinpot show that goes with it. An opera may have plenty of good music in it and fail, but if it has a good enough show it will succeed.

Such a composer as Wagner, of course, could not write even an opera without getting some music into it. In nearly all of his works, even including "Tarsifal," there are magnificent passages, and some of them are very long. Here his natural genius overcame him" and he forgot temporarily what he was about But these magnificent passages pass unnoticed by the average opera audience. What it esteems in his music dramas is precisely what is cheapest and most mounte-bankish — for example, the more lascivious parts of "Tristan und Isolde." The sound music it dismisses as tedious. The Wagner it venerates is not the musician, but the showman. That he had a king for a backer and was seduced by Liszt's daughter — these facts, and not the fact of his stupendous talent" are the foundation stones of his fame in the opera house. Greater men, lacking his touch of the quads:, have failed where he succeeded — Beethoven, Schubert, Schumann, Brahms, Bach, Haydn, Haendel. Not one of them produced a genuinely successful opera; most of them didn't even try. Imagine Brahms writing for the diamond horseshoe! Or Bach! Or Haydn! Beethoven attempted it, but made a mess of it; "Fidelio" survives to-day chiefly as a set of concert overtures. Schubert wrote more actual music every morning between 10 o'clock and lunch time than the average opera composer produces in 250 years, and yet he always came a cropper in the opera house.

3. The Music of To-morrow

Viewing the current musical scene, Carl Van Vechten finds it full of sadness. Even Debussy bores him; he heard nothing interesting from that quarter for a long while before the final scene. As for Germany, he finds it a desert, with Arnold Schoenberg behind the bar of its only inviting Gasthaus. Richard

Strauss? Pooh! Strauss is an exploded torpedo, a Zeppelin brought to earth; "he has nothing more to say." (Even the opening of the Alpine symphony, it would appear, is mere stick-candy.) England? Go to! Italy? Back to the barrel-organ! Where, then, is the tone poetry of to-morrow to come from? According to Van Vechten, from Russia. It is the steppes that will produce it — or, more specifically. Prof. Igor Strawinsky, author of "The Nightingale" and of various revolutionary ballets. In the scores of Strawinsky, says Van Vechten, music takes a vast leap forward. Here, at last, we are definitely set free from melody and harmony; the thing becomes an ineffable complex of rhythms; "all rhythms are beaten into the ears."

New? Of the future? I have not heard all of the powerful shiverings and tremblings of M. Strawinsky, but I presume to doubt it none the less. "The ancient Greeks," says Van Vechten, "accorded rhythm a

higher place than either melody or harmony." Well, what of it? So did the ancient Goths and Huns. So do the modern Zulus and New Yorkers. The simple truth is that the accentuation of mere rhythm is a proof, not of progress in music, but of a reversion to barbarism. Rhythm is the earliest, the underlying element. The African savage, beating his tom-tom, is content to go no further; the American composer of fox trots is with him. But music had scarcely any existence as an art-form until melody came to rhythm's aid, and its fruits were little save dullness until harmony began to support melody. To argue that mere rhythm, unsupported by anything save tone-color, may now take their place is to argue something so absurd that its mere statement is a sufficient answer to it.

The rise of harmony, true enough, laid open a dangerous field. Its exploration attracted meticulous minds; it was rigidly mapped in hard, geometrical forms; in the end, it became almost unnavigable to the man of ideas. But no melodramatic rejection of all harmony is needed to work a reform. The business, indeed, is already gloriously under way. The dullest conservatory pupil has learned how to pull the noses of the old-time schoolmasters. No one cares a hoot any more about the ancient laws of preparation and resolution. (The rules grow so loose, indeed, that I may soon be tempted to write a tone-poem myself) But out of this chaos new laws will inevitably arise, and though they will not be as rigid as the old ones, they will still be coherent and logical and intelligible. Already, in fact, gentlemen of professorial mind are mapping them out; one needs but a glance at such a book as Rene Lenormand's to see that there is a certain order hidden in even the wildest vagaries of the moment. And when the boiling in the pot dies down, the truly great musicians will be found to be, not those who have been most daring, but those who have been most discreet and intelligent — those who have most skillfully engrafted what is good in the new upon what was sound in the old. Such a discreet fellow is Richard Strauss. His music is modern enough — but not too much. One is thrilled by its experiments and novelties, but at the same time one can enjoy the thing as music.

Haydn, Mozart, Beethoven and Wagner belonged to the same lodge. They were by no means the wildest revolutionaries of their days, but they were the best musicians. They didn't try to improve music by purging it of any of the elements that made it music; they tried, and with success, to give each element a new force and a new significance. Berlioz, I dare say, knew more about the orchestra than Wagner; he surely went further than Wagner in reaching out for new orchestral effects. But nothing he ever wrote has a fourth of the stability and value of "'Die Meister singer" He was so intrigued by his tone-colon that he forgot his music.

4. Tempo di Valse

Those Puritans who snort against the current dances are quite right when they argue that the tango and the shimmie are violently aphrodisiacal, but what they overlook is the fact that the abolition of such provocative wriggles would probably revive something worse, to wit, the Viennese waltz. The waltz never quite goes out of fashion; it is always just around the corner; every now and then it comes back with a bang. And to the sore harassment and corruption, I suspect, of chemical purity, the ideal of all right-thinkers. The shimmie and the tango are too gross to be very dangerous to civilized human beings; they suggest drinking beer out of buckets; the most elemental good taste is proof enough against them. But the waltz! Ah, the waltz, indeed! It is sneaking, insidious, disarming, lovely. It does its work, not like a college-yell or an explosion in a munitions plant, but like the rustle of the trees, the murmur of the illimitable sea, the sweet gurgle of a pretty girl. The jazz-band fetches only vulgarians, barbarians, idiots, pigs. But there is a mystical something in "Weiner Blut" or "Kunstler Leben" that fetches even philosophers.

The waltz, in fact, is magnificently improper — the art of tone turned bawdy. I venture to say that the compositions of one man alone, Johann Strauss II, have lured more fair young creatures to lamentable complaisance than all the hyperdermic syringes of all the white slave scouts since the fall of the Western Empire. There is something about a waltz that is simply irresistible. Try it on the fattest and sedatest or even upon the thinnest and most acidulous of women, and she will be ready, in ten minutes, for a stealthy kiss behind the door — nay, she will forthwith impart the embarrassing news that her husband misunderstands her, and drinks too much, and cannot appreciate Maeterlinck, and is going to Cleveland, O., on business to-morrow. . . .

I often wonder that the Comstocks have not undertaken a crusade against the waltz. If they suppress "The 'Genius' " and "Jurgen," then why do they overlook "Rosen aus dem Suden"? If they are so hot against "Madame Bovary" and the Decameron, then why the immunity of "Wein, Weib und Gesang"? . . . I throw out the suggestion and pass on. Nearly all the great waltzes of the world, incidentally, were written by Germans — or Austrians. A waltz-pogrom would thus enlist the American Legion and the Daughters of the Revolution. Moreover, there is the Public Health Service: it is already engaged upon a campaign to enforce virginity in both sexes by statute and artillery. Imagine such an enterprise with every band free to play "Wiener Mad´l"!

5. The Puritan as Artist

The saddest thing that I have ever heard in the concert hall is Herbert K. Hadley's overture, "In Bohemia." The title is a magnificent piece of profound, if unconscious irony. One looks, at least, for a leg flung in the air, a girl kissed, a cork popped, a flash of drawer-ruffles. What one encounters is a meeting of the Lake Mohonk Conference. Such prosy correctness and hollowness, in music, is almost inconceivable. It is as if the most voluptuous of the arts were suddenly converted into an abstract and austere science, like comparative grammar or astro-physics. "Who's Who in America" says that Hadley was born in Somerville, Mass., and "studied violin and other branches in Vienna." A prodigy thus unfolds itself: here is a man who lived in Vienna, and yet never heard a Strauss waltz! This, indeed, is an even greater feat than being born an artist in Somerville.

6 The Human Face

Probably the best portrait that I have ever seen in America is one of Theodore Dreiser by Bror Nordfeldt. Who this Bror Nordfeldt may be I haven't the slightest notion — a Scandinavian, perhaps. Maybe I have got his name wrong; I can't find any Nordfeldt in "Who's Who in America." But whatever his name, he has painted Dreiser in a capital manner. The portrait not only shows the outward shell of the man; it also conveys something of his inner spirit — his simpleminded wonder at the mystery of existence, his constant effort to argue himself out of a despairing pessimism, his genuine amazement before life as a spectacle. The thing is worth a hundred Sargents, with their slick lying, their childish facility, their general hollowness and tackiness. Sargent should have been a designer of candy-box tops. The notion that he is a great artist is one of the astounding delusions of Anglo-Saxondom. What keeps it going is the patent fact that he is a very dexterous craftsman — one who understands thoroughly how to paint, just as a good plumber knows how to plumb. But of genuine aesthetic feeling the man is almost as destitute as the plumber. His portrait of the four Johns Hopkins professors is probably the worst botch ever palmed off on a helpless committee of intellectual hay and feed dealers. But Nordfeldt, in his view of Dreiser, somehow gets the right effect. It is rough painting, but real painting. There is a knock-kneed vase in the foreground, and a bunch of flowers apparently painted with a shaving-brush — but Dreiser himself is genuine.

More, he is made interesting. One sees at once that he is no common man.

The artist himself seems to hold the portrait in low esteem. Having finished it, he reversed the canvas and used the bade for painting a vapid snow scene — a thing almost bad enough to go into a Fifth Avenue show-window. Then he abandoned both pictures. I discovered the portrait by accidentally knocking the snow scene off a wall. It has never been framed. Dreiser himself has probably forgotten it . . • No, I do 710" predict that it will be sold to some Pittsburgh nail manufacturer, in 1950, for $100,000. If it lasts two or three more years, unframed and disesteemed, it will be running in luck. When Dreiser is hanged, I suppose, relic-hunters will make a search for it. But by that time it will have died as a doormat.

7. The Cerebral Mime

Of all actors, the most offensive to the higher cerebral centers is the one who pretends to intellectuality. His alleged intelligence, of course, is always purely imaginary: no man of genuinely superior intelligence has ever been an actor. Even supposing a young man of appreciable mental powers to be lured upon the stage, as philosophers are occasionally lured into bordellos, his mind would be inevitably and almost immediately destroyed by the gaudy nonsense issuing from his mouth every night. That nonsense enters into the very fiber of the actor. He becomes a grotesque boiling down of all the preposterous characters that he has ever impersonated. Their characteristics are seen in his manner, in his reactions to stimuli, in his point of view. He becomes a walking artificiality, a strutting dummy, a thematic catalogue of imbecilities.

There are, of course, plays that are not wholly nonsense, and now and then one encounters an actor who aspires to appear in them. This aspiration almost always overtakes the so-called actor-manager — that is to say, the actor who has got rich and is thus ambitious to appear as a gentleman. Such aspirants commonly tackle Shakespeare, and if not Shakespeare, then Shaw, or Hauptmann, or Rostand, or some other apparently intellectual dramatist. But this is seldom more than a passing madness. The actor-manager may do that sort of thing once in a while, but in the main he sticks to his garbage. Consider, for example, the late Henry Irving. He posed as an intellectual and was forever gabbling about his services to the stage, and yet he appeared constantly in such puerile things as "The Bells," beside which the average newspaper editorial or college yell was literature. So with the late Mansfield. His pretension, deftly circulated by press-agents, was that he was a man of brilliant and polished mind. Nevertheless, he spent two-thirds of his life in the theater playing such abominable drival as "A Parisian Romance" and "Dr. Jekyll and Mr. Hyde."

It is commonly urged in defense of certain actors that they are forced to appear in that sort of stuff by the public demand for it — that appearing in it painfully violates their secret pruderies. This defense is unsound and dishonest. An actor never disdains anything that gets him applause and money; he is almost completely devoid of that aesthetic conscience which is the chief mark of the genuine artist If there were a large public willing to pay handsomely to hear him recite limericks, or to blow a comet, or to strip off his underwear and dance a polonaise stark naked, he would do it without hesitation — and then convince himself that such buffooning constituted a difficult and elevated art, fully comparable to Wagner's or Dante's. In brief, the one essential, in his sight, is the chance to shine, the fat part, the applause. Who ever heard of an actor declining a fat part on the ground that it invaded his intellectual in! The thing is simply unimaginable.

VIII. THE CULT OF HOPE

OF all the sentimental errors which reign and rage in this incomparable republic, the worst, I often suspect, is that which confuses the function of criticism, whether aesthetic, political or social, with the function of reform. Almost invariably it takes the form of a protest: "The fellow condems without offering anything better. Why tear down without building up?" So coo and snivel the sweet ones: so wags the national tongue. The messianic delusion becomes a sort of universal murrain. It is impossible to get an audience for an idea that is not "constructive" — i. e., that is not glib, and uplifting, and full of hope, and hence capable of tickling the emotions by leaping the intermediate barrier of the intelligence.

In this protest and demand, of course, there is nothing but a hollow sound of words — the empty babbling of men who constantly mistake their mere feelings for thoughts. The truth is that criticism, if it were thus confined to the proposing of alternative schemes, would quickly cease to have any force or utility at all, for in the overwhelming majority of instances no alternative scheme of any intelligibility is imaginable, and the whole object of the critical process is to demonstrate it. The poet, if the victim is a poet, is simply one as bare of gifts as a herring is of fur: no conceivable suggestion will ever make him write actual poetry. The cancer cure, if one turns to popular swindles, is wholly and absolutely without merit — and the fact that medicine offers us no better cure does not dilute its bogusness in the slightest. And the plan of reform, in politics, sociology or what not, is simply beyond the pale of reason; no change in it or improvement of it will ever make it achieve the downright impossible. Here, precisely, is what is the matter with most of the notions that go floating about the country, particularly in the field of governmental reform. The trouble with them is not only that they won't and don't work; the trouble with them, more importantly, is that the thing they propose to accomplish is intrinsically, or at all events most probably, beyond accomplishment. That is to say, the problem they are ostensibly designed to solve is a problem that is insoluble. To tackle them with a proof of that insolubility, or even with a colorable argument of it, is sound criticism; to tackle them with another solution that is quite as bad, or even worse, is to pick the pocket of one knocked down by an automobile.

Unluckily, it is difficult for a certain type of mind to grasp the concept of insolubility. Thousands of poor dolts keep on trying to square the circle; other thousands keep pegging away at perpetual motion. The number of persons so afflicted is far greater than the records of the Patent Office show, for beyond the circle of frankly insane enterprise there lie circles of more and more plausible enterprise, and finally we come to a circle which embraces the great majority of human beings. These are the optimists and chronic hopers of the world, the believers in men, ideas and things. These are the advocates of leagues of nations, wars to make the world safe for democracy, political mountebanks, "clean-up" campaigns, laws, raids. Men and Religion Forward Movements, eugenics, sex hygiene, education, newspapers. It is the settled habit of such credulous folk to give ear to whatever is comforting; it is their settled faith that whatever is desirable will come to pass. A caressing confidence — but one, unfortunately, that is not borne out by human experience. The fact is that some of the things that men and women have desired most ardently for thousands of years are not nearer realization to-day than they were in the time of Rameses, and that there is not the slightest reason for believing that they will lose their coyness on any near to-morrow. Plans for hurrying them on have been tried since the beginning; plans for forcing them overnight are in copious and antagonistic operation to-day; and yet they continue to hold off and elude us, and the chances are that they will keep on holding off and eluding us until the angels get tired of the show, and the whole earth is set off like a gigantic bomb, or drowned, like a sick cat, between two buckets.

But let us avoid the grand and chronic dreams of the race and get down to some of the concrete problems of life under the Christian enlightenment. Let us take a look, say, at the so-called drink problem, a small sub-division of the larger problem of saying men from their inherent and incurable hoggishness. What is the salient feature of the discussion of the drink problem, as one observes it going on eternally in These States? The salient feature of it is that very few honest and intelligent men ever take a hand in the business — that the best men of the nation, distinguished for their sound sense in other fields, seldom show any interest in it. On the one hand it is labored by a horde of obvious jackasses, each confident that he can dispose of it overnight. And on the other hand it is sophisticated and obscured by a crowd of oblique fellows, hired by interested parties, whose secret desire is that it be kept unsolved. To one side, the professional gladiators of Prohibition; to the other side, the agents of the brewers and distillers. But why do all neutral and clear-headed men avoid it? Why does one hear so little about it from those who have no personal stake in it, and can thus view it fairly and accurately? Is it because they are afraid?

Is it because they are not intrigued by it? I doubt that it would be just to accuse them in either way. The real reason why they steer clear of the gabble is simpler and more creditable. It is this: that none of them — that no genuinely thoughtful and prudent man — can imagine any solution which meets the tests of his own criticism — that no genuinely intelligent man believes the thing is soluble at all.

Here, of course, I generalize a bit heavily. Honest and intelligent men, though surely not many of them, occasionally come forward with suggestions. In the midst of so much debate it is inevitable that even a man of critical mind should sometimes lean to one side or the other — that some salient imbecility should make him react toward its rough opposite. But the fact still remains that not a single complete and comprehensive scheme has ever come from such a man, that no such man has ever said, in so many words, that he thought the problem could be solved, simply and effectively. All such schemes come from idiots or from sharpers disguised as idiots to win the public confidence. The whole discussion is based upon assumptions that even the most casual reflection must reject as empty balderdash.

And as with the drink problem, so with most of the other great questions that harass and dismay the helpless human race. Turn, for example, to the sex problem. There is no half-baked ecclesiastic, bawling in his galvanized-iron temple on a suburban lot, who doesn't know precisely how it ought to be dealt with. There is no fantoddish old suffragette, sworn to get her revenge on man, who hasn't a sovereign remedy for it. There is not a shyster of a district attorney, ambitious for higher office, who doesn't offer to dispose of it in a few weeks, given only enough help from the city editors. And yet, by the same token, there is not a man who has honestly studied it and pondered it, bringing sound information to the business, and understanding of its inner difficulties and a clean and analytical mind, who doesn't believe and hasn't stated publicly that it is intrinsically and eternally insoluble. I can't think of an exception, nor does a fresh glance through the literature suggest one. The latest expert to tell the disconcerting truth is Dr. Maurice Parmelee, the criminologist. His book, 'Personality and Conduct," is largely devoted to demonstrating that the popular solutions, for all the support they get from vice crusaders, complaisant legislators and sensational newspapers, are unanimously imbecile and pernicious — that their only effect in practice is to make what was bad a good deal worse. His remedy is — what? An alternative solution? Not at all. His remedy, in brief, is to abandon all attempts at a solution, to let the whole thing go» to cork up all the reformers and try to forget it.

And in this proposal he merely echoes Havelock Ellis, undoubtedly the most diligent and scientific student of the sex problem that the world has yet seen — in fact, the one man who, above all others, has made a decorous and intelligent examination of it possible. Ellis' remedy is simply a denial of all remedies. He admits that the disease is bad, but he shows that the medicine is infinitely worse, and so he proposes going back to the plain disease, and advocates bearing it with philosophy, as we bear colds in the head, marriage, the noises of the city, bad cooking and the certainty of death. Man is inherently vile — but he is never so vile as when he is trying to disguise and deny his vileness. No prostitute was ever so costly to a community as a prowling and obscene vice crusader, or as the dubious legislator or prosecuting officer who jumps as he pipes.

Ellis, in all this, falls under the excommunication of the sentimentalists. He demolishes one scheme without offering an alternative scheme. He tears down without making any effort to build up. This explains, no doubt, his general unpopularity; into mouths agape for peruna, he projects only paralyzing streams of ice-water. And it explains, too, the curious fact that his books, the most competent and illuminating upon the subject that they discuss, are under the ban of the Comstocks in both England and America, whereas the hollow treatises of ignorant clerics and smutty old maids are merchanted with impunity, and even commended from the sacred desk. The trouble with Ellis is that he tells the truth, which is the unsafest of all things to tell. His crime is that he is a man who prefers facts to illusions, and knows what he is talking about. Such men are never popular. The public taste is for merchandise of a precisely opposite character. The way to please is to proclaim in a confident manner, not what is true, but what is merely comforting. This is what is called building up. This is constructive criticism.

IX. THE DRY MILLENNIUM

1. The Holy War

THE fact that the enforcement of Prohibition entails a host of oppressions and injustices — that it puts a premium upon the lowest sort of spying, affords an easy livelihood to hordes of professional scoundrels, subjects thousands of decent men to the worst sort of blackmail, violates the theoretical sanctity of domicile, and makes for bitter and relentless enmities, — this fact is now adduced by its ever-hopeful foes as an argument for the abandonment of the whole disgusting crusade. By it they expect to convert even a large minority of the drys, apparently on the theory that the latter got converted emotionally and hastily, and that an appeal to their sense of justice and fair-dealing will debamboozle them.

No hope could be more vain. What all the current optimists overlook is that the illogical and indefensible persecutions certain to occur in increasing number under the Prohibition Amendment constitute the chief cause of its popularity among the sort of men who are in favor of it. The typical Prohibitionist, in other words, is a man full of religious excitement, with the usual sadistic overtones. He delimits in persecution for its own sake. He likes to see the other fellow jump and to hear him yell. This thirst is horribly visible in all the salient mad mullahs of the land — that is, in all the genuine leaders of American culture. Such skillful boob-bumpers as the Rev. Dr. Billy Sunday know "at that culture is; they know what the crowd wants. Thus they convert the preaching of the alleged Word of God into a rough-and-tumble pursuit of definite sinners — saloon-keepers, prostitutes. Sabbath-breakers, believers in the Darwinian hypodiesis, German exegetes, faand-books, poker-players, adulterers, cigarette-smokers, users of profanity. It is the chase that heats up the great mob of Methodists, not the Word. And the fact that the chase is unjust only tickles them the more, for to do injustice with impunity is a sign of power, and power is the thing that the inferior man always craves most violently.

Every time the papers print another account of a Prohibitionist agent murdering a man who resists him, or searching some woman's underwear, or raiding a Vanderbilt yacht, or blackmailing a Legislature, or committing some other such inordinate and anti-social act, they simply make a thousand more votes for Prohibition. It is precisely that sort of entertainment that makes Prohibition popular with the boobery. It is precisely because it is unjust, imbecile, arbitrary and tyrannical that they are so hot for it. The incidental violation of even the inferior man's liberty is not sufficient to empty him of delight in the chase. The victims reported in the newspapers are commonly his superiors; he thus gets the immemorial democratic satisfaction out of their discomfiture. Besides, he has no great rage for liberty himself. He is always willing to surrender it at demand. The most popular man under a democracy is not the most democratic man, but the most despotic man. The common folk delight in the exactions of such a man. They like him to boss them. Their natural gait is the goose-step.

It was predicted by romantics that the arrival of Prohibition would see the American workingman in revolt against its tyranny, with mills idle and industry paralyzed. Certain boozy labor leaders even went so far as to threaten a general strike. No such strike, of course, materialized. Not a single American workingman uttered a sound. The only protests heard of came from a few barbarous foreigners, and these malcontents were quickly beaten into submission by the Polizei. In a week or two all the reserve stocks of beer were exhausted, and every jug of authentic hard liquor was emptied. Since then, save for the ghastly messes that he has brewed behind locked doors, the American workingman has been dry. Wone, he has also been silent. Not a sound has come out of him... But his liver is full of bile? He nourishes an intolerable grievance? He will get his revenge, soon or late, at the polls? All moonshine! He will do nothing of the sort. He will actually do what he always does — that is, he will make a virtue of his necessity, and straightway begin believing that he likes Prohibition, that it is doing him a lot of good, that he wouldn't be without it if he could. This is the habitual process of thou" of inferior men, at all times and everywhere. This is the sturdy common sense of the plain people.

2. The Lure of Babylon

One of the ultimate by-products of Prohibition and the allied Puritanical barbarities will probably be an appreciable slackening in the present movement of yokels toward the large cities. The thing that attracted the peasant youth to our gaudy Sodoms and Ninevehs, in the past, was not, as sociologists have always assumed, the prospect of less work and more money. The country boy, in point of fact — that is, the average country boy, the normal country boy — had to work quite as hard in the city as he ever worked in the country, and his wages were anything but princely. Unequipped with a city trade, unprotected by a union, and so forced into competition with the lowest types of foreign labor, he had to be content with monotonous, uninspiring and badly-paid jobs. He did not 'become a stock-broker, or even a plumber; until the war gave him a temporary chance at its gigantic swag, he became a car conductor, a porter or a wagon-driver. And it took him many years to escape from that sordid fate, for the city boy, with a better education and better connections, was always a lap or two ahead of him. The notion that yokels always succeed in the cities is a great delusion. The overwhelming majority of our rich men are city-born and city-bred. And the overwhelming majority of our elderly motormen, forlorn corner grocerymen, neighborhood carpenters and other such blank cartridges are country-bred.

No, it was not money that lured the adolescent husbandman to the cities, but the gay life. What he dreamed of was a more spacious and stimulating existence than the farm could offer — an existence crowded with intriguing and usually unlawful recreations. A few old farmers may have come in now and then to buy gold bricks or to hear the current Henry Ward Beechers, but these oldsters were mere trippers — they never thought of settling down — the very notion of it would have appalled them. The actual settlers were all young, and what brought them on was

less an economic impulse than an aesthetic one. They wanted to live magnificently, to taste the sweets that drummers talked of, to sample the refined divertisements described in such works as 'The Confessions of an Actress," "Night Life in Chicago" and "What Every Young Husband Should Know." Specifically, they yearned for a semester or two in the theaters, the saloons and the bordellos — particularly, the saloons and bordellos. It was this gorgeous bait that dragged them out of their barn-yards. It was this bait that landed a select few in Wall street and the United States Senate — and millions on the front seats of trolley-cars, delivery-wagons and ash-carts.

But now Puritanism eats the bait. In all our great cities the public stews are closed, and the lamentable irregularities they catered to are thrown upon an individual initiative that is quite beyond the talents and enterprise of a plow-hand. Now the saloons are closed too, and the blind-pigs begin to charge such prices that no peasant can hope to pay them. Only the theater remains — and already the theater loses its old lavish devilishness. True enough, it still deals in pornography, but that pornography becomes exclusive and even esoteric: a yokel could not under" stand the higher farce, nor could he afford to pay for a seat at a modern leg-show. The cheap burlesque house of other days is now incurably moral; I saw a burlesque show lately which was almost a dramatization of a wall-card by Dr. Frank Crane. There remains the movie, but the peasant needn't come to the city to see movies— there is one in every village. What remains, then, of the old lure? What sane youth, comfortably housed on a farm, with Theda Bara performing at the nearest cross-roads, wheat at $2.25 a bushel and milkers getting $75 a month and board — what jejune rustic, not downright imbecile, itches for the city to-day?

3. Cupid and Well-Water

In the department of amour, I daresay, the first effect of Prohibition will be to raise up impediments to marriage. It was alcohol, in the past, that was the primary cause of perhaps a majority of alliances among civilized folk. The man, priming himself with cocktails to achieve boldness, found himself suddenly bogged in sentimentality, and so yielded to the ancient tricks of the lady. Absolutely sober men will be harder to snare. Coffee will never mellow them sufficiently. Thus I look for a fall in the marriage rate.

But only temporarily. In the long run. Prohibition will make marriage more popular, at least among the upper classes, than it has ever been in the past, and for the plain reason that, once it is in full effect, the life of a civilized bachelor will become intolerable. In the past he went to his club. But a club without a bar is as hideously unattractive as a beautiful girl without hair or teeth. No sane man will go into it. In two years, in fact, nine out of ten clubs will be closed. The only survivors will be a few bleak rookeries for senile widowers. The bachelor of less years, unable to put up with the society of such infernos, will inevitably decide that if he must keep sober he might just as well have a charming girl to ease his agonies, and so he will expose himself in society, and some fair one or other will nab him.

At the moment, observing only the first effect of Prohibition, the great majority of intelligent women are opposed to it. But when the secondary effect begins to appear they will become in favor of it. They now have the vote. I see no hope.

4. The Triumph of Idealism

Another effect of Prohibition will be that it will gradually empty the United States of its present small minority of civilized men. Almost every man that one respects is now casting longing eyes across the ocean. Some of them talk frankly of emigrating, once Europe pulls itself together. Others merely propose to go abroad every year and to stay there as long as possible, visiting the United States only at intervals, as a Russian nobleman, say, used to visit his estates in the Ukraine. Worse, Prohibition will scare off all the better sort of immigrants from the other side. The lower order of laborers may continue to come in small numbers — each planning to get all the money he can and then escape, as the Italians are even now escaping. But no first-rate man will ever come — no Stephen Girard, or William Osier, or Carl Schurz, or Theodore Thomas, or Louis Agassiz, or Edwin Klebs, or Albert Gallatin, or Alexander Hamilton. It is not Prohibition per se that will keep them away; it is the whole complex of social and political attitudes underlying Prohibition — the whole clinical picture of Puritanism rampant. The United States will become a sort of huge Holland — fat and contented, but essentially undistinguished. Its superior men will leave it automatically, as nine-tenths of all superior Hollanders leave Holland.

But all this, from the standpoint of Prohibitionists, is no argument against Prohibition. On the contrary, it is an argument in favor of Prohibition. For the men the Prohibitionist — i. e., the inferior sort of Puritan — distrusts and dislikes most intensely is precisely what the rest of humanity regards as the superior man. You will go wrong if you imagine that the honest yeomen of, say, Mississippi deplore the fact that in the whole state there is not a single distinguished man. They actually delist in it. It is a source of genuine pride to them that no suck irreligious scoundrel as Balzac lives there, and no such scandalous adulterer as Wagner, and no scoundrelly atheist as Huxley, and no such rambunctious piano-thumper as Beethoven, and no such German spy as Nietzsche. Such men, settling there, would be visited by a Vigilance Committee and sharply questioned. The Puritan Commonwealth, now as always, has no traffic with heretics.

X. APPENDIX ON A TENDER THEME

1. The Nature of Love

WHATEVER the origin (in the soul, the ductless glands or the convolutions of the cerebrum) of the thing called romantic love, its mere phenomenal nature may be very simply described. It is, in brief, a wholesale diminishing of disgusts, primarily based on observation, but often, in its later stages, taking on an hallucinatory and pathological character. Friendship has precisely the same constitution, but the pathological factor is usually absent. When we are attracted to a person and find his or her proximity agreeable, it means that he or she disgusts us less than the average human being disgusts us — which, if we have delicate sensibilities, is a good deal more than is comfortable. The elemental man is not much oppressed by this capacity for disgust; in consequence, he is capable of falling in love with almost any woman who seems sexually normal. But the man of a higher type is vastly more sniffish, and so the majority of women whom he meets are quite unable to interest him, and when he succumbs at last it is always to a woman of special character, and often she is also one of uncommon shrewdness and enterprise.

Because human contacts are chiefly superficial" most of the disgusts that we are conscious of are physical. We are never honestly friendly with a man who is dirtier than we are ourselves, or who has table manners that are cruder than our own (or merely noticeably different), or who laughs in a way that strikes us as gross, or who radiates some odor that we do not like. We never conceive a romantic passion for a woman who employs a toothpick in public, or who suffers from acne, or who offers the subtle but often quite unescapable suggestion that she has on soiled underwear. But there are also psychical disgusts. Our friends, in the main, must be persons who think substantially as we do, at least about all things that actively concern us, and who have the same general tastes. It is impossible to imagine a Brahmsianer being honestly fond of a man who enjoys jazz, or a man who admires Joseph Conrad falling in love with a woman who reads Rex Beach' By the same token, it is impossible to imagine a woman of genuine refinement falling in love with a Knight of Pythias, a Methodist or even a chauffeur; either the chauffeur is a Harvard aviator in disguise or the lady herself is a charwoman in disguise. Here, how ever, the farce of aversion may be greatly diminished by contrary physical attractions; the body, as usual, is enormously more potent than the so-called mind. In the midst of the bitterest wars, with every man of the enemy held to be a fiend in human form, women constantly fall in love with enemy soldiers who are of pleasant person and wear attractive uniforms. And many a fair agnostic, as every one knows, is on good terms with a handsome priest • • •

Imagine a young man in good health and easy circumstances, entirely ripe for love. The prompting to mate and beget arises within his interstitial depths, traverses his lymphatic system, lifts his blood pressure, and goes whooping through his *meatus auditorium externus* like a fanfare of slide trombones' The impulse is very powerful. It staggers and dismays him. He trembles like a stag at bay. Why, then, doesn't he fall head over heels in love with the first eligible woman that he meets? For the plain reason that the majority of women that he meets offend him, repel him, disgust him. Often it is in some small, inconspicuous and, at first glance, unanalyzable way. She is, in general, a very pretty girl — but her ears stand out too much. Or her hair reminds him of oakum. Or her mouth looks like his aunt's. Or she has beer-keg ankles. Here very impalpable things, such as bodily odors, play a capital part; their importance is always much underestimated.

Many a girl has lost a husband by using the wrong perfume, or by neglecting to have her hair washed. Many another has come to grief by powdering her nose too much or too little, or by shrinking from the paltry pain of having some of her eyebrows pulled, or by employing a lip-salve with too much purple in it, or by patronizing a bad dentist, or by speaking incautiously of chilblains. . • .

But eventually the youth finds his love — soon or late the angel foreordained comes along. Who is this prodigy? Simply the first girl to sneak over what may be called the threshold of his disgusts — simply the first to disgust him so little, at first glance, that the loud, insistent promptings of the Divine Schadchen have a chance to be heard. If he muffs this first, another will come along, maybe soon, maybe late. For every normal man there are hundreds of thousands in Christendom, thousands in his own town, scores within his own circle of acquaintance. This normal man is not too delicate. His fixed foci of disgust are neither very numerous nor very sensitive. For the rest, he is swayed by fashion, by suggestion, by transient moods. Anon a mood of cynicism is upon him and he is hard to please, but anon he succumbs to sentimentality and is blind to everything save the grossest off endings. It is only the man of extraordinary sensitiveness, the man of hypertrophied delicacy, who must search the world for his elective affinity.

Once the threshold is crossed emotion comes to the aid of perception. That is to say, the blind, almost irresistible mating impulse, now fortuitously relieved from the contrary pressure of active disgusts, fortifies itself by manufacturing illusions. The lover sees with an eye that is both opaque and out of focus. Thus he begins the familiar process of editing and improving his girl. Features and characteristics that, observed in cold blood, might have quickly aroused his most active disgust are now seen through a rose-tinted fog, like drabs in a musical comedy. The lover ends by being almost anaesthetic to disgust. While the spell lasts his lady could shave her head or take to rubbing snuff, or scratch her leg at a communion service, or smear her hair with bear's grease, and yet not disgust him. Here the paralysis of the faculties is again chiefly physical — a matter of obscure secretions, of shifting pressure, of metabolism. Nature is at her tricks. The fever of love is upon its victim. His guard down, he is little more than a pathetic automaton. The shrewd observer of gaucheries, the sensitive sniffer, the erstwhile cynic, has become a mere potential papa.

This spell, of course, doesn't last forever. Marriage cools the fever and lowers the threshold of disgust. The husband begins to observe that the lover was blind to, and often his discoveries affect him as unpleasantly as the treason of a trusted friend. And not only is the fever cooled: the opportunities for exact observation are enormously increased. It is a commonplace of juridical science that the great majority of divorces have their origin in the connubial chamber. Here intimacy is so extreme that it is fatal to illusion. Both parties, thrown into the closest human contact that either has suffered since their unconscious days in utero, find their old capacity for disgust reviving, and then suddenly flaming. The girl who was perfect in her wedding gown becomes a ghastly caricature in her *robe de nuit*; the man who was a Chevalier Bayard as a wooer becomes a muffling, shambling, driveling nuisance as a husband— a fellow offensive to eyes, ears, nose, touch and immortal soul. A learned judge of my acquaintance, constantly hearing divorce actions and as constantly striving to reconcile the parties, always tries to induce plaintiff and defendant to live apart for a while, or, failing that, to occupy separate rooms, or, failing that, to at least dress in separate rooms. According to this jurist, a husband who shaves in his wife's presence is either an idiot or a scoundrel. The spectacle, he argues, is intrinsically disgusting, and to force it upon a refined woman is either to subject her to the most exquisite torture or to degrade her gradually to the insensate level of an *Abortfrau*.

The day is saved, as every one knows, by the powerful effects of habit The acquisition of habit is the process whereby disgust is overcome in daily life — the process whereby one may cease to be disgusted by a persistent noise or odor. One suffers horribly at first, but after a bit one suffers less, and in the course of time one scarcely suffers at all. Thus a man, when his marriage enters upon the stage of regularity and safety, gets used to his wife as he might get used to a tannery next door, and vice versa. I think that women, in this direction, have the harder row to hoe, for they are more observant than men, and vastly more sensitive in small ways. But even women succumb to habit with humane rapidity, else every marriage would end in divorce. Disgusts pale into mere dislikes, disrelishes, distastes. They cease to gag and torture. But though they thus shrink into the shadow, they are by no means disposed of. Deep down in the subconscious they continue to lurk, and some accident may cause them to flare up at any time, and so work havoc. This flaring up accounts for a familiar and yet usually very mystifying phenomenon — the sudden collapse of a marriage, a friendship or a business association after years of apparent prosperity.

2. The Incomparable Buzzsaw

The chief (and perhaps the only genuine) charm of women is seldom mentioned by the orthodox professors of the sex. I refer to the charm that lies in the dangers they present. The allurement that they hold out to men is precisely the allurement that Cape Hatteras holds out to sailors: they are enormously dangerous and hence enormously fascinating. To the average man, doomed to some banal and sordid drudgery all his life long, they offer the only grand hazard that he ever encounters. Take them away and his existence would be as flat and secure as that of a milch-cow. Even to the unusual man, the adventurous man, the imaginative and romantic man, they offer the adventure of adventures. Civilization tends to dilute and cheapen all other hazards. War itself, once an enterprise stupendously thrilling, has been reduced to mere caution and calculation; already, indeed, it employs as many press-agents, letter-openers, and chautauqua orators as soldiers. On some not distant to-morrow its salient personality may be Potash, and if not Potash, then Perlmutter. But the duel of sex continues to be fought in the Berserker manner. Whoso approaches women still faces the immemorial dangers. Civilization has not made them a bit more safe than they were in Solomon's time; they are still inordinately barbarous and menacing, and hence inordinately provocative, and hence inordinately charming and romantic

The most disgusting cad in the world is the man who, on grounds of decorum and morality, avoids the game of love. He is one who puts his own ease and security above the most laudable of philanthropies. Women have a hard time of it in this world. They are oppressed by man-made laws, man-made social customs, masculine egoism, the delusion of masculine superiority. Their one comfort is the assurance that, even though it may be impossible to prevail against man, it is always possible to enslave and torture a man. This feeling is fostered when one makes love to them. One need not be a great beau, a seductive catch, to do it effectively. Any man is better than none. No woman is ever offended by admiration. The wife of a millionaire notes the reverent glance of a head-waiter. To withhold that devotion, to shrink poltroonishly from giving so much happiness at such small expense, to evade the business on the ground that it has hazards — this is the act of a puling and tacky fellow.

3. Women as Spectacles

Women, when it comes to snaring men, throng the eye, bait a great many hooks that fail to fluster the fish. Nine-tenths of their primping and decorating of their persons not only doesn't please men; it actually repels men. I often pass two days running without encountering a single woman who is charmingly dressed. Nearly all of them run to painful color schemes, absurd designs and excessive over-ornamentation. One seldom observes a man who looks an absolute guy, whereas such women are very numerous; in the average theater audience they constitute a majority of at least nine-tenths. The reason is not far to seek. The clothes of men are plain in design and neutral in hue. The only touch of genuine color is in the florid blob of the face, the center of interest — exactly where it ought to be. If there if any other color at all, it is a faint suggestion in the cravat — adjacent to the face, and so leading the eye toward it. It is color that kills the clothes of the average woman. She runs to bright spots that take the eye away from her face and hair. She ceases to be woman clothed and becomes a mere piece of clothing womaned.

Even at the basic feminine art of pigmenting their faces very few women excel. The average woman seems to think that she is most lovely when her sophistication of her complexion is most adroitly concealed — when the *poudre de riz* is rubbed in so hard that it is almost invisible, and the penciling of eyes and lips is perfectly realistic. This is a false notion. Most men of appreciative eye have no objection to artificiality *per se,* so long as it is intrinsically sightly. The marks made by a lip-stick may be very beautiful; there are many lovely shades of scarlet, crimson and vermilion. A man with eyes in his head admires them for themselves; he doesn't have to be first convinced that they are non-existent, that what he sees is not the mark of a lip-stick at all, but an authentic lip. So with the eyes. Nothing could be more charming than an eye properly reenforced; the naked organ is not to be compared to it; nature is an idiot when it comes to shadows. But it must be admired as a work of art, not as a miraculous and incredible eye. . . . Women, in this important and venerable art, stick too closely to crude representation. They forget that men do not admire the technique, but the result. What they should do is to forget realism for a while, and concentrate their attention upon composition, chiaroscuro and color.

4. Woman and the Artist

Much gabble is to be found in the literature of the world upon the function of woman as inspiration, stimulant and *agente provocateuse* to the creative artist. The subject is a favorite one with sentimentalists, most of whom are quite beyond anything properly describable as inspiration, either with or without feminine aid. I incline to think, as I hint, that there is little if any basis of fact beneath the theory. Women not only do not inspire creative artists to high endeavor; they actually stand firmly against every high endeavor that a creative artist initiates spontaneously. What a man's women folks almost invariable ask of him is that he be respectable — that he do something generally approved — that he avoid yielding to his aberrant fancies — in brief, that he sedulously eschew showing any sign of genuine genius. Their interest is not primarily in the self-expression of the individual, but in the well-being of the family organization, which means the safety of themselves. No sane woman would want to be the wife of such a man, say, as Nietzsche or Chopin. His mistress perhaps, yes — for a mistress can always move on when the weather gets too warm. But not a wife. I here speak by the book. Both Nietzsche and Chopin had plenty of mistresses, but neither was ever able to get a wife.

Shakespeare and Ann Hathaway, Wagner and Minna Planer, Moliere and Armande Bejart — one might multiply instances almost endlessly. Minna, at least in theory, knew something of music; she was thus what romance regards as an ideal wife for Wagner. But instead of helping him to manufacture his incomparable masterpieces, she was for twenty-five years the chief impediment to their manufacture. "Lohengrin" gave her the horrors; she begged Richard to give up his lunacies and return to the composition of respectable comet music. In the end he had to get rid of her in sheer self-defense. Once free, with nothing worse on his hands than the illicit affection of Cosima Liszt von Bulow, he produced music drama after music drama in rapid succession. Then, married to Cosima, he descended to the anticlimax of "Parsifal," a truly tragic mixture of the stupendous and the banal, of work of genius and *sinfonia domestica* — a great man dying by inches, smothered by the smoke of French fried potatoes, deafened by the wailing of children, murdered in his own house by the holiest of passions.

Sentimentalists always bring up the case of Schumann and his Clara in rebuttal. But does it actually rebut? I doubt it. Clara, too, perpetrated her attentat against art. Her fair white arms, lifting from the keyboard to encircle Robert's neck, squeezed more out of him than mere fatuous smirks. He had the best head on him that music had seen since Beethoven's day; he was, on the cerebral side, a colossus; he might have written music of the very first order. Well, what he did write was piano music — some of it imperfectly arranged for orchestra. The sad eyes of Clara were always upon him. He kept within the limits of her intelligence, her prejudices, her wifely love. No grand experiments with the orchestra. No superb leapings and cavortings. No rubbing of sandpaper over critical ears. Robert lived and died a respectable musical Hausvater. He was a man of genuine genius — but he didn't leave ten lines that might not have been passed by old Prof. Jadassohn.

The truth is that, no matter how great the domestic concord and how lavish the sacrifices a man makes for his women-folk, they almost always regard him secretly as a silly and selfish fellow, and cherish the theory that it would be easily possible to improve him. This is because the essential interests of men and women are eternally antithetical. A man may yield over and over again, but in the long run he must occasionally look out for himself — and it is these occasions that his women-folk remember. The typical domestic situation shows a woman trying to induce a man to do something that he doesn't want to do, or to refrain from something that he does want to do. This is true in his bachelor days, when his mother or his sister is his antagonist. It is preeminently true just before his marriage, when the girl who has marked him down is hard at the colossal job of overcoming his reluctance. And after marriage it is so true that there is hardly need to state it. One of the things every man discovers to his disquiet is that his wife, after the first play-acting is over, regards him essentially as his mother used to regard him — that is, as a self -worshiper who needs to be policed and an idiot who needs to be protected. The notion that women admire their men-folks is pure moonshine. The most they ever achieve in that direction is to pity them. When a woman genuinely loves a man it is a sign that she regards him much as a healthy man regards a one-armed and epileptic soldier.

5. Martyrs

Nearly the whole case of the birth-controllers who now roar in Christendom is grounded upon the doctrine that it is an intolerable outrage for a woman to have to submit to motherhood when her private fancies may rather incline to automobiling, shopping or going to the movies. For this curse the husband is blamed; the whole crime is laid to his swinish lasciviousness. With the highest respect, nonsense! My private suspicion, supported by long observation, copious prayer and the most laborious cogitation, is that no woman delights in motherhood so vastly as this woman who theoretically abhors it. She experiences, in fact, a double delight. On the one hand, there is the caressing of her vanity — a thing enjoyed by every woman when she achieves the banality of viable offspring. And on the other hand, there is the fine chance it gives her to play the martyr — a chance that every woman seeks as diligently as a man seeks ease. All these so-called unwilling mothers wallow in their martyrdom. They revel in the opportunity to be pitied, made much over and envied by other women.

6. The Burnt Child

The fundamental trouble with marriage is that it shakes a man's confidence in himself, and so greatly diminishes his general competence and effectiveness. His habit of mind becomes that of a commander who has lost a decisive and calamitous battle. He never quite trusts himself thereafter.

7. The Supreme Comedy

Marriage, at Best, is full of a sour and inescapable comedy, but it never reaches the highest peaks of the ludicrous save when efforts are made to escape its terms — that is, when efforts are made to loosen its bonds, and so ameliorate and denaturize it. All projects to reform it by converting it into a free union of free individuals are inherently absurd. The thing is, at bottom, the most rigid of existing conventionalities, and the only way to conceal the fact and so make it bearable is to submit to it docilely. The effect of every revolt is merely to make the bonds galling, and, what is worse, poignantly obvious. Who are happy in marriage? Those with so little imagination that they cannot picture a better state, and those so shrewd that they prefer quiet slavery to hopeless rebellion.

8. A Hidden Cause

Many a woman, in order to bring the man of her choice to the altar of God, has to fight him with such relentless vigilance and ferocity that she comes to hate him. This, perhaps, explains the unhappiness of many marriages. In particular, it explains the unhappiness of many marriages based upon what is called "love."

9. Bad Workmanship

The essential slackness and incompetence of women, their congenital incapacity for small expertness, already descanted upon at length in my psychological work, "In Defense of Women," is never more plainly revealed than in their manhandling of the primary business of their sex. If the average woman were as competent at her trade of getting a husband as the average car conductor is at his trade of robbing the fare-box, then a bachelor beyond the age of twenty-five would be so rare in the world that yokels would pay ten cents to gape at him. But women, in this fundamental industry, pursue a faulty technique and permit themselves to be led astray by unsound principles. The axioms into which they have precipitated their wisdom are nearly all untrue. For example, the axiom that the way to capture a man is through his stomach — which is to say, by feeding him lavishly. Nothing could be more absurd. The average man, at least in England and America, has such rudimentary tastes in victualry that he doesn't know good food from bad. He will eat anything set before him by a cook that he likes. The true way to fetch him is with drinks. A single bottle of drinkable wine will fill more men with the passion of love than ten sides of beef or a ton of potatoes. Even a Seidel of beer, deftly applied, is enough to mellow the hardest bachelor. If women really knew their business, they would have abandoned cooking centuries ago, and devoted themselves to brewing, distilling and bartending. It is a rare man who will walk five blocks for a first rate meal. But it is equally a rare man who, even in the old days of freedom, would not walk five blocks for a first-rate cocktail. To-day he would walk five miles.

Another unsound feminine axiom is the one to the effect that the way to capture a man is to be distant — to throw all the burden of the courtship upon him. This is precisely the way to lose him. A man face to face with a girl who seems reserved and unapproachable is not inspired thereby to drag her off in the manner of a caveman; on the contrary, he is inspired to thank God that here, at last, is a girl with whom it is possible to have friendly doings without getting into trouble — that here is one not likely to grow mushy and make a mess. The average man does not marry because some marble fair one challenges his enterprise. He marries because chance throws into his way a fair one who repels him less actively than most, and because his delight in what he thus calls her charm is reenforced by a growing suspicion that she has fallen in love with him. In brief, it is chivalry that undoes him. The girl who infallibly gets a husband — in fact, any husband that she wants — is the one who tracks him boldly, fastens him with sad eyes, and then, when his conscience has begun to torture him, throws her arms around his neck, bursts into maidenly tears on his shoulder, and tells him that she fears her forwardness will destroy his respect for her. It is only a colossus who can resist such strategy. But it takes only a man of the intellectual grade of a Y. M. C. A. secretary to elude the girl who is afraid to take the offensive.

A third bogus axiom I have already discussed, to wit, the axiom that a man is repelled by palpable cosmetics — that the wise girl is the one who effectively conceals her sophistication of her complexion. What could be more untrue? The fact is that very few men are competent to distinguish between a layer of talc and the authentic epidermis, and that the few who have the gift are quite free from any notion that the latter is superior to the former. What a man seeks when he enters the society of women is something pleasing to the eye. That is all he asks. He does not waste any time upon a chemical or spectroscopic examination of the object observed; he simply determines whether it is beautiful or not beautiful. Has it so long escaped women that their husbands, when led astray, are usually led astray by women so vastly besmeared with cosmetics that they resemble barber-poles more than human beings? Are they yet blind to the superior pull of a French maid, a chorus girl, a stenographer begauded like a painter's palette? . . . And still they go on rubbing off their varnish, brushing the lampblack from their eyelashes, seeking eternally the lip-stick that is so depressingly purple that it will deceive! Alas, what folly!

End of Second Series

Made in the USA
Monee, IL
15 July 2020

36522704R00059